The Wreath Book

This book is for Micah

Editor: Dawn Cusick
Design and Production: Thom Boswell
Typesetting: Diane Deakin
Photographer: Martin Fox

Special thanks to all the wreath designers, particularly to Kate Jayne, Fairman
Jayne, Fred Gaylor, and Claudette Stewart for their ongoing assistance.

10   9   8   7   6   5   4   3   2

A Sterling/Lark Book

First paperback edition published in 1995 by
Sterling Publishing Company, Inc.
387 Park Avenue South, New York, N.Y. 10016

Produced by Altamont Press, Inc.
50 College Street, Asheville, NC 28801

© 1988 by Rob Pulleyn

Distributed in Canada by Sterling Publishing
   % Canadian Manda Group, One Atlantic Avenue, Suite 105
   Toronto, Ontario, Canada M6K 3E7

Distributed in Great Britain and Europe by Cassell PLC
   Wellington House, 125 Strand, London WC2R 0BB, England

Distributed in Australia by Capricorn Link (Australia) Pty Ltd.
   P.O. Box 6651, Baulkham Hills, Business Centre, NSW 2153, Australia

Every effort has been made to ensure that all the information in this book is
accurate. However, due to differing conditions, tools, and individual skills, the
publisher cannot be responsible for any injuries, losses, and other damages which
may result from the use of the information in this book.

Sterling ISBN 0-8069-6842-7 Trade
            0-8069-6841-9 Paper

The Wreath Book

by Rob Pulleyn

Sterling Publishing Co., Inc.   New York

A STERLING/LARK BOOK

The subtle progression of color in this wreath makes an attractive design scheme. Dried German statice, Queen Anne's lace, globe amaranth, candytuft, sarrecena lilies, and roses were glued to a 16-inch (41-cm.) grapevine base.

contents

introduction

Almost all of us can conjure up images of a wreath from the potpourri of our childhood memories. At the very least, we remember the holiday wreath that joyously adorned the front door during the Christmas season, with its fragrant evergreen boughs, crisp pine cones, and bright red bow.

The use of wreaths to celebrate and decorate goes back much further than our own childhoods. In the ancient cultures of Persia, Parthia, and Artemia, a wreath was called a **diadem**, from the Greek word **diadema**, which means ``a thing bound around.'' Diadems were bands of fabric worn around the brow of a royal bonnet, and they symbolized royalty.

Wreaths made of various leaves were used as prizes during the Greek Olympics. Each host city would award head garlands made of its local trees, such as olive and laurel. Thus originated the olive leaf as a peace symbol and the phrase, ``to earn your laurels.''

To the Romans, the Greek royal headdresses were seen as symbols of despotic power. Diadems were an insult to their high regard for democracy and were fervently shunned. However, the Roman fascination with these headdresses was not totally squelched and soon the upper classes were wearing garlands of oak leaves and laurel. These head wreaths became symbols of military and athletic prowess, and were worn with great pride. When Julius Caesar became leader, the Romans promptly crowned their victorious general with a wreath of fresh laurel.

Diadems and head wreaths did not go unnoticed by the world's elite, and soon the upper classes of other countries were designing royal headdresses of their own. Precious jewels and metals were added, eventually creating the ornate crowns we have come to associate with royalty. In fact, the word ``crown'' derives from the Latin word **corona**, meaning garland or wreath. When the concept of a crown as a symbol for royalty was firmly seated in tradition, during the 15th century, the working classes began searching for a headdress of their own. It wasn't long before all social classes began wearing wreaths to celebrate different occasions and to honor religious holidays.

Plants were a natural choice for wreath ingredients. Almost every ancient culture worshipped trees as symbols of divine energy, and arrangements of boughs and sprigs embodied both secular and religious meaning. Holly, mistletoe, and other evergreens, for example,

The wreath to the left welcomes guests from its home on an old garden gate. Made from an assortment of dried weeds and grasses from the garden, it has small strawflowers sprinkled throughout for added color. Below, an old herbal wreath has been lovingly pinned to a rustic backroads fence, to be admired by those who wander by.

A bright red door is the dramatic background for this subdued arrangement of dried flowers, primarily German statice, strawflowers, and wisps of dried ferns. Below, colorful dyed flat reed has been wrapped around a straw base. Delicate sprays of baby's breath have been added to create a modern welcome for a traditional oak entry door.

were brought indoors to shelter the sylvan spirits from the cold of winter. A woman who accepted the advances of a lover gave him a crown of birch; if rejected, he received a crown of hazel. Because the circle symbolizes eternity, the wreath also became a natural and fitting addition to funerals.

Exactly when the transition from "wreath as head ornament" to "wreath as wall decoration" occurred is unclear, but it is quite possible that someone who was so enamored with a festival headdress hung it up on a wall instead of throwing it away.

The process of putting this book together has been fascinating — from learning the history of wreaths to discovering how wreaths are used today. No longer do we see wreaths limited to the front door or over the fireplace. A beautiful deep-toned wreath of dried flowers or herbs is as appropriate in a formal living room as a Christmas wreath is on the front door. Holiday season wreaths of evergreen and pine cones are still popular, and in fact we devote several chapters to this tradition, but we also wanted to share with you the rich variety of wreath styles and designs being made today.

An interesting aspect of contemporary wreaths is function. While those of the classical past were essentially symbolic in nature and those of the Victorian era were purely decorative, many of the wreaths in this book actually serve a practical purpose. You will find wreaths made into napkin holders, air fragrancers, and spice racks. You also will discover edible wreaths, jewelry, and display cases for treasured colectibles.

Still another exciting discovery is how a wreath itself can reflect the creative style and personality of its maker. The wreath designers who contributed to this book are diverse — they are nurserymen, floral designers, and even the 12-year-old daughter of the author. However, they all have one very important thing in common: a simple love for their materials and a heartfelt joy in making wreaths.

When you begin making your own wreaths you will be amazed to discover yet another design style — your own. Even when you try to duplicate one of the designs in this book, you will undoubtedly make some subtle changes, add different ingredients, or rearrange their order. Enjoy your personalized interpretation of these wreath designs and be assured that it's difficult to make an ugly wreath. If you're not delighted by the results of a particular wreath project, simply add a few new ingredients to perk it up or just remove the elements from your base and start again. Above all, have fun making your wreath discoveries.

various bases

Every wreath owes its beginning to a base (sometimes called a frame), and consequently the importance of choosing the right base can't be underestimated. Some crucial considerations are: How will the wreath's design elements be attached to the base? How heavy are the elements? And, will the base serve as an integral part of the wreath's design?

Bases made of natural materials — such as moss, twigs, straw, dried husks, shredded wood or vines — are great for elements that are inserted with wires, pins or picks. Partially exposed, they can be a handsome part of the wreath's overall design. They can also be partially wrapped in ribbon or given a light spray of grey or white paint for extra color.

While single, double or two-dimensional wire or reinforced styrofoam bases are sturdier than their natural counterparts, they are not attractive in themselves and should be completely covered.

If you plan to glue your elements on, be sure to test how well your base holds glue before you begin. A glue gun may cause a styrofoam base to melt.

The wide variety of bases available (both commercially and homemade) may seem confusing at first, but with a little experimentation you'll soon be a pro. The only steadfast rule is to always choose a base worthy of the time and effort you plan to invest in your wreath.

Specialty bases are also available. The green base in the lower left, for instance, holds water for living materials such as ivy, while the smooth brown base on the top right is foam covered with crushed cinnamon and spices to emit a pleasant fragrance from the finished wreath.

useful tools

The number and sophistication of tools used in wreathmaking is minimal.

Besides a hot glue gun (purchased at a crafts or hardware store), floral wire, tape, picks and pins (purchased from a florist's shop), the only tools really necessary to make a beautiful wreath are wire snips, a ruler, and a small pair of pliers. Other tools helpful in wreathmaking can be found scattered around your home. Some, like hairspray, may be found on the dressing table, spray polyurethane in the basement, or white glue in the ubiquitous kitchen junk drawer. We have chosen not to photograph shiny new tools, fresh from their boxes, but instead the real ones used by the wreathmakers in this book. The strange item on the top left is a wreath hanger which hooks over a door.

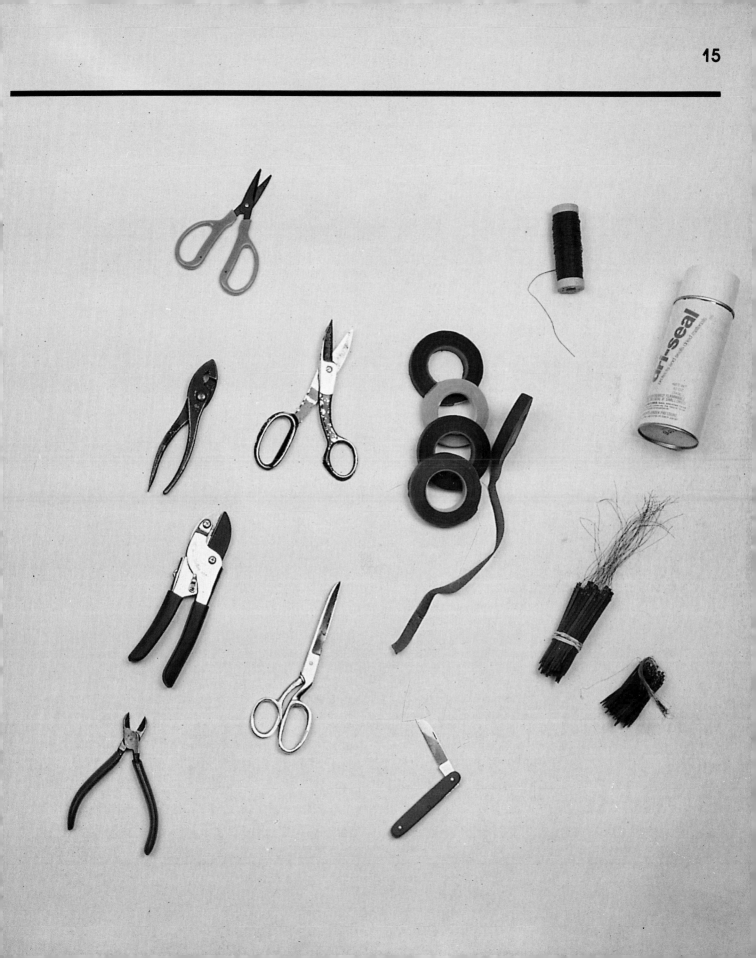

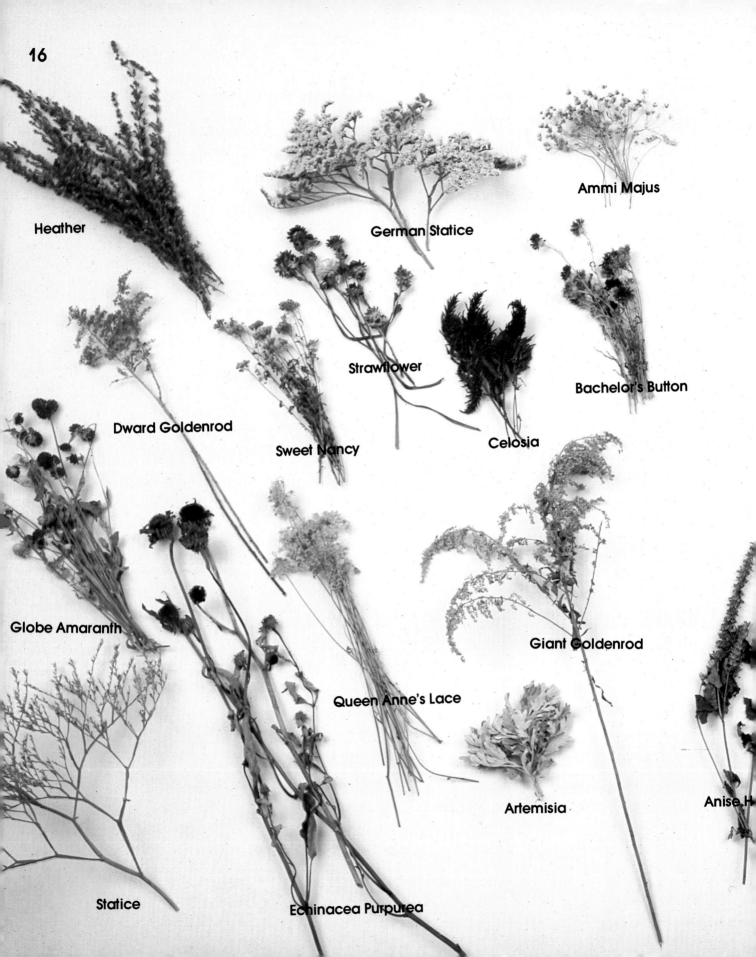

Heather

German Statice

Ammi Majus

Strawflower

Bachelor's Button

Sweet Nancy

Celosia

Dward Goldenrod

Globe Amaranth

Giant Goldenrod

Queen Anne's Lace

Artemisia

Anise H

Statice

Echinacea Purpurea

flowers & herbs

Nothing quite matches the beauty of a floral wreath. Shown here is an assortment of dried flowers and herbs used to make many of the wreaths in this book. They can be purchased at floral shops or grown at home. Don't be intimidated by the apparent scarcity of dried herbs; they're frequently available from health food stores or through mail order suppliers.

Billows of German statice or baby's breath are common backgrounds for delicate roses, bright globe amaranth, colorful strawflowers, or dramatic celosia.

Pictured here are the most popular and common ingredients of floral and herbal wreaths; none of them is difficult to find or grow, although you'll certainly want to include those special flowers and herbs natural to your area in your own wreaths.

But beware: even if you're not a gardener, making wreaths of dried flowers and herbs will surely implant in you the urge to create a small garden spot where you can watch your own flowers and herbs blossom.

Red Clover

Feverfew

Baby's Breath

Marigold

Rabbit Tobacco

Statice Sinuata

Old Rose

Queen Anne's Lace

White Yarrow

Zinnia

Leaf Yarrow

wildflowers, grasses & seeds

While flowers provide the color, and herbs the aroma, nothing adds drama and texture to a wreath like wildflowers, grasses, and seed heads.

These materials grow along roadsides, abandoned lots, and even in your own yard. Their natural beauty should encourage you to consider rearranging your gardening priorities. We might even suggest you let a small portion of your lawn grow wild. You'll be surprised what beautiful materials are simply mowed down every week or two. And, if anyone should complain, give them a wreath containing some elements from your wild garden.

Many of these materials can also be found in wet areas near streams or rivers, along ditches, or near construction sites. When you open your eyes to beauty, you'll find it in abundance.

fascinating fakes

Maybe we shouldn't tell you, but nothing pictured here is real. Plastics and silks have come a long way since the days when you could tell at twenty paces that something was just not right with an arrangement. The textures were wrong, the colors were off, the structures too perfect.

Even though the bias of this book is toward naturals, there's plenty of room for well-made fakes. They allow you to make Christmas wreaths that will last through the season, or to have fun with silk vegetables and flowers in dramatic arrangements. Several of the wreaths in this book compromise between natural and fake, using silk garlands of evergreens to cover a base and then adding dry or fresh flowers. The plastic materials are easily cleaned, although special care must be taken when cleaning silk items.

As an alternative to using fakes, many natural ingredients can be spray painted to give them color, but this should be done carefully to avoid inappropriate shiny surfaces or colors.

Floral and craft shops are good sources for these fabulous fakes. Look for the best quality materials, as the quality of the materials will be reflected in your finished wreath.

evergreens & cones

When most of us think of wreaths, we think of an arrangement of evergreen boughs sprinkled with bright red berries or perhaps a tightly made wreath of pine cones. From small hemlock cones to majestic cedar boughs, the range of these coniferous materials is tremendous, and they all make handsome wreaths.

wiring flowers

Fresh and dried flowers — whether they're used as accents or make up an entire wreath — are valuable design tools to any wreathmaker. The strength of their beauty, though, is generally accompanied by a weakness in their stems. And since flowers are inserted into wreath bases by their stems, it's imperative their stems be strengthened. This strengthening is easily accomplished with the aid of floral wire.

Floral wire is available in pre-cut lengths or on spools, and comes in a variety of widths. You'll also need a pair of wire cutters or florist's scissors and a roll of floral tape in a compatible shade of green or brown.

Begin by cutting a length of wire about twice as long as the stem. Wrap the wire around the top of the stem several times to secure it, and continue wrapping down the stem at a 45° angle. Allow several inches (4 - 7 cm.) of wire to hang past the natural stem. The wire is then wrapped in floral tape, using the same procedure.

For very delicate flowers, such as helichrysums, trim the stem to 1½ inches (3.5 cm.). Hold a length of heavy-gauge wire parallel with the natural stem, and wrap both the stem and the wire together with a thin-gauge wire.

For stems that are thick and unattractive, or for stems just too delicate to wire, the natural stem can be replaced with a sturdier, more flexible wire stem. Push a length of medium-gauge wire through the center of the flower's head from the back side. Continue pushing the wire through the head until you have enough length to make a small hook. Then pull the wire back down so the hook securely embeds in the flower head.

Cones and other large items can also be attached to a wreath base with great alacrity and ease using wire. Wiring in these large items (as opposed to attaching them with glue) also allows you much more flexibility in the design process. Just wire your elements in place, hang the wreath, and stand back and study the effect. Then, if you're not pleased with the results, the items can be removed or relocated in a matter of minutes — without damage to the items or your base.

To wire a cone, simply fold a length of heavy-gauge wire in half and slip the looped end down around one of the cone's lower scales. Twist the wire ends together and fold the scales of the cone back to cover the wire. If the cones are going into a tight arrangement (such as an all-cone wreath), the wires won't show and you won't have to cover them with floral tape. In wreaths where the cones are used as accents, though, the wires will probably show and need taping.

To wire other larger items — such as Christmas ornaments, stuffed animals, bows, etc. — the only challenge is in finding an inconspicuous place to attach the wire. A bow can be wired in after it's finished (usually through a loop in the ribbon in the back), or before the bow's been made when it's still a long strand of ribbon.

picking clusters

Many times the beauty of a single small flower is diluted when inserted by itself into a wreath base. By wiring two to four stems together, however, even the most delicate beauties will be noticed. Wiring materials into bunches also gives you a greater variety of design possibilities. Clumps of evergreen, for example, can be wired together with a branch of holly berries in the center.

The wiring process is the same for single flowers and bunches. Use medium- to heavy-gauge wire, and clump items together with similar stem lengths. (Remember that natural stems can always be lengthened with wire.) Be sure to wire the stems together very tightly to ensure a compact stem that will easily insert into a base. Wrap the wired stems with floral tape, unless you're inserting them into a moss-covered base or other wispy material that will conceal the wire.

The easiest and quickest means of inserting bunches of material into a base is to use floral picks. They are short sticks pointed at one end with fine wire attached to the blunt end. To use them, place the pick so that it extends about one-half of the pick's length beyond the end of the stems. Wrap the fine wire around the stems and pick. Continue wrapping at a 45° angle beyond the end of the stem, so that you are eventually only wrapping the fine wire around the wooden pick. With practice, you will become adept at making picks in a matter of seconds, turning the pick and stem in one hand while holding the wire in the other.

Another type of pick is metal, used in pick machines, which automatically clamp the bunches together. Their cost is out of the range of the ordinary weekend wreathmaker, but may be available for rental from a florist.

Unfortunately, many people view stem-wiring and picking as a boring task, and consequently rarely use flowers. Make the time you spend wiring stems both productive and enjoyable by using this time to really study the detail of your flowers and to mentally play with design options.

**Floral Taped
Wooden Picks**

Wooden Picks

Metal Picks

making a wreath

Simply, a wreath is an arrangement of materials in a circle. The materials may or may not be affixed to a formal base, although the wreaths in this book all use bases. (A garland of flowers can, for instance, be brought into a circle and a baseless wreath is formed.) The use of a base generally makes stronger, longer lasting wreaths.

While you'll now learn the basics of making a wreath, the secret, if any, to a handsome wreath is not as much in the mechanics of construction — or even the tools used — but in your use of interesting, harmonious materials. Once you have, for instance, an assortment of dried flowers, it's difficult not to produce a good-looking wreath.

The first consideration when making a wreath is the materials you will be using. This determines the type and size of the base you should use. As a general guideline, the larger the elements, (gourds, seed pods, or pine cones, for example) the larger the base should be to ensure the finished wreath has a pleasant sense of balance and proportion.

Without getting ahead of ourselves, the next consideration should be what kinds of bases are available to you. Your local florist or crafts supply store may only have a narrow range of bases to choose from, (which is not necessarily bad) or you may want to make your own base. (See instructions beginning on page 29) In

either case, choose a base that's the right size for your proposed wreath. Size should also be determined by how much material you have available. If you're determined to make a wreath from this year's scanty supply of the statice you lovingly grew in a window box. You should find a base small enough to allow you to make a full wreath with your limited supply of materials.

Next, you want to consider how you'll be affixing your materials. If you intend to glue your materials to the base, you'll want a base that will easily take the glue and which provides enough surface area for gluing. Avoid bases made from twisted, thin vines — there just isn't enough surface area for the glue to adhere properly.

If you plan to use picks, either made at home or professionally, find a base that easily accepts them. Some heavy vine bases will work fine, as will straw bases. If you plan to wire your material, as you would with pine boughs, look for a base that gives you something strong to tie onto, such as a metal ring

base or a heavy vine base.

Another consideration is keeping a portion of the base exposed. Many beautiful wreaths incorporate the base into the design, as with many grapevine wreaths; or a portion of the base is wrapped in moss or artemisia. Nowhere is it written that your materials must completely cover the base. A one- or two-thirds application of materials can make a splendid wreath.

Keep in mind that after you've applied your materials to the base the wreath will be much "fuller" than the original base's size. The exact amount of this size increase will vary, depending on the type of base and the size and length of the materials you're using. Generally, though, the size of the finished wreath will be 4 to 8 inches (10 - 20 cm.) larger than the base.

Consider, too, how much the finished wreath will weigh, based on the materials you intend to use. Obviously, a dried flower wreath will rarely be heavy enough to place significant strain on a base, but using fresh gourds, shells, or fresh fruit and nuts will produce a heavy wreath and necessitate a strong, stout base. When buying a styrofoam base for such a wreath, check to

make sure it's reinforced on the inside with heavy wire; otherwise one sad morning you may find a sagging, crumpled wreath staring up at you from the floor.

Lastly, consider where your finished wreath will hang. If you're making a dried flower wreath that will hang out of reach of little hands, dust, and direct sunlight, any base will work fine. A wreath of pine cones, on the other hand, intended to hang outdoors in the elements, should be made with a weatherproof base with stronger than usual wire. A wreath designed to hang on a front door with a storm door should use a base without too much depth.

We'll say it in other places in this book, but don't think of your wreaths as lasting forever. You'll quickly realize that the wreathmaking process is almost as enjoyable as receiving one as a gift or living with one in your home. If you think your wreath should be handed down from generation to generation, you'll certainly have heirs wondering what your intentions could possibly have been in giving them a dusty, faded wreath. Instead, hand down this book, with notes in the margins about the wonderful wreaths you made way back when.

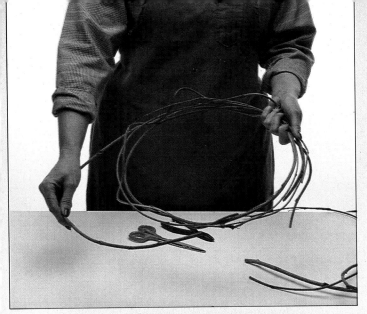

Virtually any type of vine or root makes a nice base, although grape, wisteria, and honeysuckle are most common. If the vines aren't fresh, soak them in water until they're pliable. Then begin by picking out two to four pieces of vine in various lengths, approximately 2 to 5 feet (61 - 152 cm.) with the butt ends staggered slightly 1 to 3 inches (2½ - 7½ cm.) apart Then take your vine lengths and bring them around to form a circle that's about the size of the base you wish to make. (Don't worry if one or two of the vines aren't long enough.)

Holding the vine circle in one hand, begin wrapping the longest vine around the circle, catching any shorter lengths as you go. If you want a base with more volume, choose a new starting point and add additional vines, wrapping them in the same direction. After you've added each length of vine, tuck the end in. (Note: some wreathmakers like to add additional vines in the opposite direction. Experiment to find your own preference.) Tuck in any loose tendrils if you wish (although some people like the look of stray tendrils). If necessary, clip any unsightly pieces.

straw base

Decide first on the circumference of the wreath you wish to make. Any type of straw-like material will work — hay, dried grass, or alfalfa, for example. Take a handful of the straw (or other material) and compress it until it's about 1½ inches (4 cm.) thick. The length should be about 1 foot (31 cm.), with one end dense and the other slightly tapered. Begin wrapping the straw with heavy spooled floral wire, adding new straw as necessary to maintain the correct thickness. Make sure the wire is pulled tight and the wraps are about 1 inch (2½ cm.) apart.

Continue this process until you have a "snake" approximately the circumference you chose. Bring the "snake" around to form a circle and overlap about 6 inches (15 cm.) of straw onto the beginning of your "snake." Continue to wrap until you have gone beyond the original starting point about 6 inches (15 cm.) and wrap all the way around one more time, keeping your wire wrappings about 1 inch (2½ cm.) apart. Don't worry about the loose ends as you're wrapping — they can be tucked in or trimmed after the base is finished. Finally, pull and push your wreath base until it's molded into the circular shape you desire.

Because the fibers in moss are not as strong as those of straw and vine, a moss base must be secured around a strong, central core. A commercially available metal wire frame works well, or you can easily make your own ring with the metal wire from a sturdy coat hanger. If you're making your own frame, begin by cutting the wire the length of your planned wreath's circumference, plus about 4 inches (10 cm.). With a pair of pliers, bend back 2 inches (5 cm.) on both ends of the wire. Attach the floral wire to the base. Then, place a handful of dried moss at one end of the base and wrap the floral wire around the moss several times to secure it. Place additional clumps of moss on the frame and wrap it securely, overlapping each new clump of moss, maintaining a width of approximately 2 inches (5 cm.).

Wrap the wire very tightly so the moss will be able to withstand the pressure of floral picks or pins. Once you've reached the end, bring the two ends of the wire together, hooking them into a circle using the overlaps. Cover the hooked wire with moss and continue wrapping for approximately 6 more inches (15 cm.). Secure the floral wire. At this point, you can easily make aesthetic adjustments in both the thickness and shape by molding the moss with your hands.

Some of the most beautiful wreaths in this book are made of dried flowers; and yet, ironically, they're one of the simplest wreaths to make. The example here is a straw base covered with moss. This combination of straw and moss makes a fuller wreath and allows the moss to function as part of the design. The moss is placed around the base in clumps, and secured with floral pins.

1. Start with a straw or moss base with the plastic or tape covering removed.

2. Have ready your clusters of materials. They can be individually prepared flowers (usually saved for the final step), picked or wired clusters of flowers, or clusters you intend to pin to the base. Generally, a cluster is made up of 3 to 5 sprigs of flowers.

3. Put your first clusters on top of the wreath and insert them into the base with pins or picks. Continue placing the clusters around the top of the wreath, leaving 1 to 2 inches (5 cm.) of each cluster exposed as you add each new one. Always work in one direction, turning the base as you go.

Another popular method is to cover the inner and outer edges of the base first, usually with a single flower or grass type, such as caspia or German statice. The top of the base is covered last, usually with a variety of materials. (Several wreaths in the Dried Flower chapter, pages 72-81, are made this way.)

If you're using a variety of flowers, make sure you don't overuse any particular color in one area, unless that's your intention. Space any "special" clusters around the wreath, paying attention not to be overly symmetrical. (Designer tip: to ensure even flower distribution, mentally divide the wreath into four or five units. Pretend each unit is a separate wreath and insert your flowers accordingly.)

4. Attach the last cluster by lifting up the first cluster and attaching it underneath. Repeat steps 1 and 2 around the outside and inside of the wreath so that the entire surface of the wreath base is covered with material.

5. Look over your wreath to make sure you've covered the base. Clip any errant flowers that disrupt the symmetry of your design. You may add single accent flowers now, or other decorations, including a bow. Stand back and enjoy your creative handiwork.

While many materials can be attached to a frame or base by using pins or wire, it doesn't make much sense to do so when you can glue the elements onto the base. While a wired element may have a better chance of living through a decade of use, the glues available today closely rival the longevity of wire — and they're much faster to use. Combining wire and glue is also an option, and means a particularly strong wreath.

When using glue, it's important that the glue has a good surface to adhere to. This means a surface that is clean, dry, and able to absorb enough glue to form a secure bond.

The best type of glue to use is milk-based. These glues, going by such brand names as Elmers™ and Sobo™, are readily available in all manner of shops. They're easy to use, dilute well, dry almost clear, and have no toxic properties.

The shell wreath shown here is made on a straw base, using a glue gun. (The glue dries very quickly with a glue gun.)

1. Start by dividing your materials into categories by color, size, shape, texture, or any other property applicable to your wreath. In this case, the shells were divided by size, with some large, special shells placed on the wreath first in prime locations. The smaller shells were saved to be put on last.

2. Start applying your materials to the top of the base, and then begin work on the base's outside circle. Repeat this process on the inside surface of the base. Be careful not to go too far around the sides of the base to ensure the wreath will hang flat against the wall. With this wreath, medium sized shells were applied randomly after the larger shells, then the smaller shells were added.

3. Fill in any open areas with smaller bits of material or with larger, more dramatic bits of material you've saved. Add a bow if you wish.

shells glued onto straw

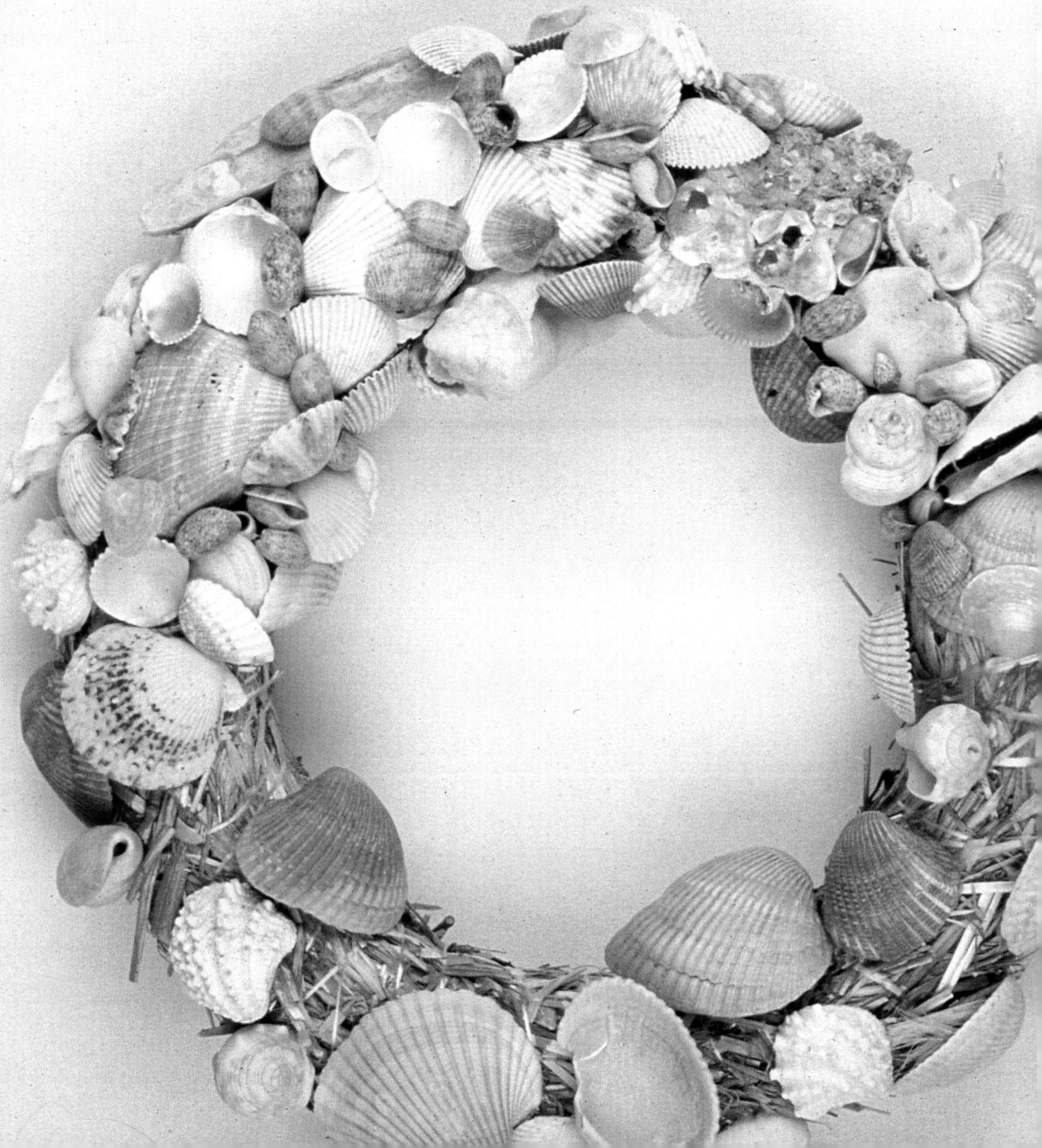

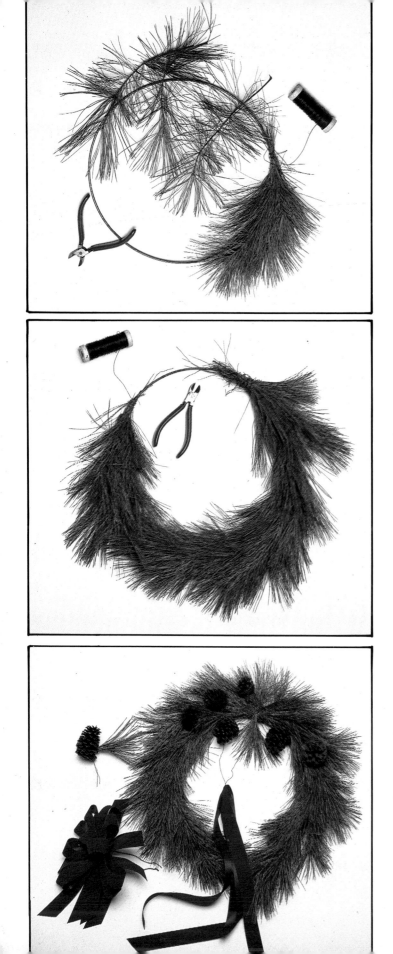

These instructions are appropriate for a wreath using large clusters of material, heavy material, or boughs of white pine, holly, hemlock, arbor vitae, red cedar, or similar materials. The base can be flat or three-dimensional, but the process is the same.

1. Assemble your materials first: one spool of medium-gauge wire; a pair of wire cutters; clusters of 3 to 6 sprigs, each one 4 - 6 inches (15 cm.) long. (Note: the larger your base, the longer the lengths of clusters it can attractively accommodate.) The pine clusters do not have to be pre-wired; we'll do that as we go along.

Securely wrap the end of the spooled wire around the base. Do not cut the wire.

2. Place a cluster of sprigs on the frame. Wrap the wire tightly several times around the cut ends of the sprigs and then around the wire frame. Again, do not cut the wire.

3. Using another cluster of sprigs, overlap the first cluster, placing the new cluster 2 - 3 inches (5 - 8 cm.) down from the previous cluster.

Follow Step 2 again, wrapping the wire around the cluster and then around the metal frame. Continue this process until you've gone all the way around the frame. An alternative method (shown in this example), is to go one-half way around the frame in one direction, and then go back to the starting point and go in the other direction.

4. If going in one direction, attach the last cluster of greens by lifting the first cluster and wiring it underneath. For either method, after wiring the last cluster to the frame, cut the wire, leaving 1 or 2 inches (2½ - 5 cm.) to wrap around the frame. Clip any out-of-place sprigs; add any special decorations (such as ornaments, sprigs of bittersweet, or fruit, especially important if using the two-direction design); and attach a hanging loop. Call in the neighbors to admire your work.

5. If you're using a three-dimensional frame, attach clusters to the top surface of the form, following the instructions above. Then repeat the process around the inside and outside surfaces of the frame.

6. If you wish to attach a bow, simply slip a wire through the back of the bow and tie it to the base.

Naturally Simple

Nothing is quite as beautiful as something simple and direct, free from unnecessary embellishment. As in cooking, good wreathmaking goes hand-in-hand with the ability to say no to just one more ingredient. Our insecurities with our aesthetic abilities often make us think that by adding more "stuff" we'll hide all the flaws and the world will find us clever.

The secret, if there is one, is to stop when you're ahead. Simply find a material that interests you and make a wreath from it. It really is that simple. The wreaths shown here are just to whet your appetite. Almost every material used in wreathmaking works beautifully alone — one color of a dried flower, unadorned pine boughs, nuts, pine cones, or even seashells — so don't be afraid to experiment.

The shell wreath here is the result of a child's unused, unseen, and almost unloved shell collection amassed over several visits to the beach. (Who has ever been able to leave the beach without a few mementos in the form of shells?) The wreath was started with a 16-inch (41-cm.) straw base with the plastic wrapping intact. The larger shells were attached first with a glue gun. Then the medium-sized shells were glued on. This procedure was done first along the top of the wreath and then on the inside and outside surfaces. Smaller shells were then added to conceal any glimmers of plastic tape. Finally, some interested observers donated some of their own beach mementos to create the final prize. The wreathmaking process was rather short — less than six hours — and now the 12-year-old designer has an heirloom remembrance of her sunny beach days.

A schoolgirl's collection of shells was finally put to use with this ingenious use of aquatic throwaways. The shells were glued to a straw base.

Naturally

Ground pine was collected and brought home to make this simple, elegant wreath, shown left. Other greens could have been used as successfully, particularly sprigs of boxwood, hemlock, ivy or other dense green.

Right, a wreath made from fresh pine is still attractive and fragrant after it dries

Simple

The ground pine wreaths shown left and below are simply a massing of natural materials over a straw base. The ground pine was inserted with picks, each one holding a small clump. Once again, the beauty of the wreath is in its simplicity. With about three pounds (6½ kg.) of material in the wreath, it is quite compact, and although the wreath will eventually turn brown and fragile, some light misting will slow the process down. This wreath would be magnificent for the holidays, and could be embellished with bows or Christmas ornaments.

As an experiment, the designer decided to make another wreath of the same size, this time adding some dried herbs. The addition made for quite a different looking wreath, and hopefully you'll do some of your own experimenting.

A simple ground pine wreath has been embellished with artemisia, rosemary and salvia, inserted after the base wreath was completed.

Naturally Simple

This silk ivy looks right at home around a base of Spanish moss. The simple bows were made of raffia.

The lushness of deep green ivy was made into the wreath below by clustering short pieces of silk ivy on wooden picks and then inserting the picks into a 12-inch (31-cm.) Spanish moss base. Strings of raffia were then tied into bows around the ivy, and small pieces of moss were tucked into the bare spots.

Nuts have always been a traditional addition to harvest wreaths. They are handsome, long lasting, and add a color and shine to an otherwise dull wreath. Here, a small 6-inch (15-cm.) wreath, which could surround a candle on a table, has been made from nuts and dried peach pits. Recycling at its best! The pits

Peach pits, chestnuts, and almonds were wired to a plywood base to make this handsome, small wall wreath that is equally beautiful as a table decoration with a large candle.

were simply washed and left outside to dry and bleach some. Along with the nuts, they were drilled and wired to a plywood or masonite base. (They could just as easily have been glued.) As you can see, elegance does not always have to come from elegant materials.

Frequently we awe at the beauty of a wheat field. But, like looking at a verdant forest, we sometimes lose the ability to appreciate a single shaft of wheat, a single tree. This

wreath, made simply from wheat stalks and oats, makes us consider the golden color and curving shape of the grass. The wreath could just as successfully have been made with other grasses and grains, many of which are assuredly available to you within a few minutes of your home, even if you live in a large city. The wreath will last for years and be a welcome addition to a bedroom, living area, or entrance to a kitchen.

The simple beauty of curving wheat stalks and oats makes an easy yet elegant wreath.

Wild Vine Wreaths

No wreath material is easier to work with or has more general appeal than grapevines. No doubt much of this appeal for grapevine wreaths comes from the ease with which they're made and their abundant supply in wooded areas everywhere. The first explorers to visit North America confronted so many thickets of wild grapevines that they immediately named the new land Vineland.

Above, a bright red bird (formerly a Christmas tree ornament) perches in a colorful cluster of dried material.

Below, a kitty (made from plywood) sits contentedly on a vine base with the curling tendrils left intact.

Although the vine can be cut and used any time of year if the leaves have been stripped off, the best time to collect grapevines is in the autumn, after the leaves have fallen and the vine is turning brown. For vines that aren't used immediately, an overnight soak in water will make them more maleable.

There are several ways to make a grapevine wreath. The easiest is to cut several stout lengths (four to eight feet; one to three meters) of vine and simply twist the sections around themselves until they hold their wreath shape. For finer lengths of grapevine, it may be necessary to support the shape as you're twisting by using wire, twine, or additional lengths of grapevine wrapped around the wreath in the opposite direction.

Most people leave their grapevine in its natural state, and smart designers never underestimate the visual interest of small, curling vine tendrils. The addition of worldly products, however, can have an almost elegant effect.

Light frostings of spray paint (grey and white are preferred) or light sprays of lacquer are frequently added.

The "country look" of grapevine is no more apparent than the wreath to the right which is the background for a home-made doll, complete with apron. On her lap sits a small painted duck, made from a scrap of wood painted with primer and acrylic paints. A small teddy bear and a child's block finish off the setting. The last-minute touches of excelsior and a hemp bow enhance the country ambiance.

The two wreaths on this page also use grapevine bases as frames for small still lifes. The upper wreath uses dried elements and a bird (purchased as a Christmas tree decoration) that's held in place with floral tape-covered wire. The designer chose to make these wreaths from thicker grapevines, which gives the base a sparser look and doesn't over-power the still life. In the wreath below it, a curious

A true country collectable.
A simple rag doll in primi-
tive dress resides in comfort
on a bed of excelsior.
Natural twine holds the
wreath together.

kitten made from a small cut-out scrap of wood perches on a palm frond, also made from scrap wood. Dried flowers and a country print bow are the final touches.

As an homage to itself, a wreath of grapevines bedecked with artificial grape bunches is a simple yet sophisticated use of materials. The first wreath starts with an 18-inch (46-cm.) grapevine base spraypainted with a light layer of grey color to contrast the grapes. The bow and streamers were wired to the base first, and then the silk grapes and leaves were wired on, being careful to keep the illusion of grapes hanging from a vine.

The natural look of a 12-inch (31-cm.) grapevine base blends well with most dried elements, especially herbs. Here lamb's ear, strawflower, annual statice, peach gomphrena, nigella pod, and bee balm were arranged on the base with white glue. The flowers were attached first and then the foliage was filled in.

Colorful dried flowers and herbs were glued to a small vine base for a simple yet lovely wreath.

Left, the fruit returns to the vine along with streamers and a bow. The grapevine was sprayed lightly with gray paint.

Wild Vine Wreaths

The carefree look of dried bittersweet combines well with a fine grapevine base. The stray tendrils were retained to give dimension to the wreath. The paper bow is fun and simple to make (see page 136 for bow making instructions), and complements the wreath nicely.

For the wreath opposite, the trumpet (in this case, a faux one created as a Christmas decoration) was first wired to the base. Then grapes, berries, blue spruce branches, small flowers (all silk), and rolled sheet music were hot glued into place, with the bow wired on last. The grey/gold ribbon helps coordinate the brass trumpet and the frosted base.

Left, branches of dried bittersweet weave in and out of a fine grapevine base.

Right, a trumpet was borrowed from a Christmas tree ornament and wired to a vine base along with small flowers, foliage, and fruit.

A glorious display of fruits
of the harvest, this wreath
features a simple wicker
cornucopia that has been
dyed to match the root
base. The basic format of
the wreath can be used at
other times to spill forth
dried flowers, or other
natural dried materials.

Harvest Wreaths

Whether you live high above a sprawling city or down the road in a country cottage, autumn has a special meaning for all of us. Traditionally, autumn is a time for bringing people together in local fairs and festivals to celebrate the produce of summer. Harvest wreaths celebrate this tradition by using gourds, apples, seed pods, brightly colored leaves, dried corn and grapes as design elements.

The cornucopia is the traditional symbol for harvests. Here it spills forth the bounty of another year in the fields and vineyards, anticipating a good year ahead. The wicker cornucopia was wired to a 17-inch (43-cm.) root base. Then a piece of styrofoam was wired into the cornucopia and the wreath base. Next the flat materials and streamers of calico ribbon were added to give the composition its shape. The larger elements — gourds, plastic grapes, and silk apples — were added next with picks, and those placed against the base were also hot glued. Small elements, such as preserved leaves, more calico ribbon, Spanish moss, and okra pods were added to fill out the wreath.

A celebration of gourds, they were first glued to a straw base and finished off with dried sunflowers, celosia and zinnias. This wreath can also be used as an intriguing centerpiece on the traditional harvest table.

The simplest homage to the harvest time is this gourd-sampler wreath. The gourds were attached to an 11-inch (28-cm.) straw frame with hot glue. Flowers were added between the gourds for simple color. Because the wreath is made from fresh gourds it is quite heavy, and extra attention should be paid with well-placed glue to ensure a good hold. The wreath will brown over time, but the result is equally beautiful.

The wreath to the right is an homage to the road-side stand, a traditional sight along country highways. On an 18-inch (46-cm.) base, sprays of bittersweet were first added with hot glue. Before glueing, they were sprayed with a clear lacquer to help set the berries on the bittersweet — otherwise they tend to fall off easily. (Other materials, such as the gourds, were also lacquered to help preserve them.) Tied bundles of Indian corn were then wired on the wreath. Next, the gourds were added with wooden picks and then hot glued onto the base for additional strength. As a final touch, bits of Spanish moss were placed around the gourds, and streamers of raffia were added.

Small gourds, sprays of
bittersweet, small ears of
Indian corn, and
sprinklings of. Spanish
moss pay homage to the
glories of autumn.

Holiday Wreaths

If you were to ask the typical non-aficianado of wreaths to describe what first came to mind when you mentioned wreaths, chances are they'd describe the typical Christmas wreaths that hang on so many front doors, festooned with the typical silver tree ornaments and bright red bows. It's a welcoming symbol in modern times, and the Christmas season is usually the only time we see homes decorated with wreaths.

Left, steal a kiss from a special person under a wreath of mistletoe.

Right, the vibrant red and green colors in this wreath come from silk fruit and foliage and small items pillaged from tree ornaments.

While the winter holidays are the traditional time for wreaths, we encourage you to think of wreaths for other holidays as well, and to think beyond the mundane types of wreaths we see everywhere. This is a gentle prod to all of you who are looking in this book for the type of wreath that Madge and Warren bought last year. You — and they — can do better.

What would Christmas be without mistletoe? Sometimes difficult to locate each winter, and being quite poisonous, we used plastic mistletoe. The first step was tying a 2-foot (61-cm.) piece of ribbon around the top of the 7-inch (18-cm.) vine base for the hanger. The hanger was then concealed with a bow, streamers, and a festive bell.

The celebration of Christmas red and green, at right, was made from a 14-inch (36-cm.) re-inforced styrofoam base onto which silk frazier fir branches and apples were inserted with wire. The wreath could have been finished off with a green and red bow, but instead the designer continued, wiring in wooden musical instruments (taken from tree ornaments), rolled sheet music, and satin ribbons.

If you're in possession of heirloom ornaments too delicate for the tree, consider adding them to a Christmas wreath where they can safely be displayed.

A celebration of the Christmas table is reflected in the assortment of fruits and berries into this wreath: grapes, blueberries, and plums. A dramatic lace and gros grain ribbon highlights this 28-inch (71-cm.) wreath.

Holiday Wreaths

The designer of this heirloom wreath started with a 24-inch (61-cm.) reinforced styrofoam base and then added pine and fir. The bow, made from 6 yards (5½ meters) of lace and gros grain ribbon was worked into the wreath as it was being made.

The designer of the wreath at right has a special fondness for potpourri and antiques, and found a way to incorporate both these interests into a wreath. The wreath started by wiring silk garland to a 22-inch (56-cm.) straw base. The horse transformed from ordinary to unique when a layer of potpourri was glued on, with Spanish moss added to highlight the mane and tail. The doll was then glued to the horse 'and the horse was wired to the base. (The doll's dress was made from antique fabrics.) Christmas balls, candles, bows, cinnamon sticks, and dried roses were wired in, with touches of gold glitter and artificial snow sprayed on for the final effect.

If you have a special hobby or fascination, do invest the extra time to find ways of incorporating it into your wreaths — it's a wonderful way to create tomorrow's heirlooms.

An elegant holiday wreath was formed by attaching red bows, tree ornaments, dried roses, cinnamon sticks, and an equestrian doll to a straw base covered with silk garland.

A Christmas wreath in the traditional red and green was highlighted by lacquered apples, available as Christmas tree decorations. The wreath started as a 14-inch (36-cm.) reinforced styrofoam base to which bleached silk pine was attached with picks. The apples were also added with picks and then secured with hot glue. Dried berries and silk holly round out the wreath.

Ah, the turning of tables. A happy bear family reminisces their latest hunt as they prepare to begin a holiday concert. A 36-inch (91-cm.) reinforced styrofoam base was wrapped and glued with 10 yards (9-m.) of velvet ribbon. Next, the "Merry Christmas" banner was lettered with a stencil and added with wire. (Covering the wire first with green floral tape keeps the wire unobtrusive.) The large musical instruments (two French horns and a trumpet) were then wired in place. Then the fun began — using floral taped wire, an assortment of other decorations was added on, saving the bears and their small musical instruments for last.

Above, a wreath of bleached evergreen boughs is adorned with plastic red apples, berries, and a bow.

Right, a 36-inch (91-cm.) styrofoam base was wrapped in red velvet ribbon to form a perch for this happy bear family.

The wreath below conjures up images of turn of the century Victorian Christmases, with its muted colors, delicate embellishments, and the porcelain doll perched on the edge, watching the festivities below. The doll was attached with wire, and the greens are not real, so this wreath easily becomes a permanent keepsake.

A subtle Victorian-style keepsake doll was wired onto a lace-wrapped straw base. Small horns, toy alphabet blocks, and small bouquets of painted cones and berries were added.

This Easter wreath is sure to be a hit with family and friends. A cherubic bunny peeks out from a springtime composition. The wreath started when a ceramic piece was glued to a 16-inch (41-cm.) grapevine base. Small pieces of foam were then wired to the front of the figure and to both sides. The foam was covered with moss, and various dried materials were inserted into it: pods first, then silk ferns, dried yarrow, peach silk flowers and statice. A ribbon of raffia finished off the piece.

An Easter bunny nests happily in a vine base. Bright dried flowers and silk ferns give the wreath a springtime aura.

Pine Cone Wreaths

Pine cones — one of nature's most beautiful throwaways — make wonderful wreaths. And because they come in so many varieties, sizes, and shapes, the design possibilities are endless. Pine cones are generally easy to find, but if you have trouble finding the variety and quantity you need, check with neighborhood kids who almost always have unappreciated collections or with craft supply stores who often sell them in bulk.

This glorious 24-inch (61-cm.) pine cone wreath was made from a variety of cones, nuts, and seed pods. The wreath's heart shape comes from a wire ring base.

Because of the relatively large size of pine cones, these wreaths go together quickly, giving you extra time to experiment with ribbons, flowers, nuts, and other decorative acumen. (They make an ideal project for restless children.) And, if you become bored with the simple shapes of pine cones, try cutting the cones horizontally to make pine cone flowers. Pine cone wreaths make easy transformations through the seasons — just add fresh holly, greenery, or change a bow.

An arabesque of nuts dramatically enhanced this 24-inch (61-cm.) pine cone wreath. The cones were wired to a heart-shaped wire base and moss was tucked into the bare spots. Instead of the traditional bow, the wreath is highlighted with a colorful bird in its nest.

Another way to add color to a cone wreath is with dried materials. At left, dried red clover and German statice combined with horse chestnuts, sweet gum tree pods, pine cone flowers, and other assorted nuts and hulls form a lively medley on the wreath's inner edge. The nuts, pods, and flowers were attached with wire and the dried elements were glued on after the outer edge of pine cones had been wired to a 12-inch (30-cm.) wire base.

Red clover and German statice add color and texture to this wreath of horse chestnuts, pine cone flowers, nuts, and seed pods.

If you like your wreaths with a little more color, consider dying some of your natural materials. At right, star and button flowers were dyed red and blue for an interesting color effect. About 30 wired pine cones were wired first to the outer edge of a 14-inch (36-cm.) wire base. The inner edge of the wreath was filled in with wired pods and more cones, and sprayed with a polyurethane finish. After the finish had dried, an assortment of dyed flowers, wheat, and wood shavings was arranged and added with glue, with the bow added last as a final touch.

Dried button and star flowers were dyed red and blue to add color to a wreath of natural browns.

At left, acorns, buckeyes, cotton husks, and gum tree balls were intermixed with pine cones for a unique effect. The outer row of larger cones was wired first to a 16-inch (41-cm.) double wire ring base. The inner row of smaller cones was wired on next, with gum tree balls, cotton husks, and pine cone flowers glued on for embellishment. The arrangement of fir and pine foliage, cones, and a plaid bow was wired on last and reinforced with hot glue.

The stunning cone wreath below began with a 16-inch (41-cm.) styrofoam base covered with sheet moss using hot glue. The cones were attached with wooden picks, and then hot-glued for reinforcement. After the cones were sprayed with a clear lacquer, an arrangement of German statice, artificial berries, gold rye, and ribbons was added with hot glue.

Cotton husks, gum tree balls, buckeyes, and acorns make beautiful accents for this wreath of solid pine cones.

CONES TO USE

Any pine cone makes a beautiful addition to a wreath. If you plan to make a long-lasting wreath (they'll easily last 15 or 20 years if well cared for), dip the cones in water before using to remove dirt and bugs; then bake them at 200° F (93° C) for 30 minutes to melt the resin; finally, after you've finished your wreath, spray them with clear lacquer or a wood-tone paint for a fresh finish. Some of the favorite cones to use are:

pine	cypress	hemlock
redwood	pinon	juniper
spruce	sequoia	fir
cedar	arbor vitae	

SEED PODS

The list of useful seed pods is literally pages long. Any growing thing which throws off a seed pod at the end of the season is fair game for a wreath. While some are more dramatic than others, they can all make wonderful additions to your wreath. Some popular pods are:

honey locust	dogwood	yucca
magnolia	wisteria	iris
rose hips	palms	corn
garlic	scotch broom	pussy willow
onion	chive	sweetgum
tulip	carrot	acorns

Wiring each row of pine cones in a different direction gives this wreath a three-dimensional look. The vibrant bouquet is made of German statice, gold rye, and artificial berries.

68

Wrapping a plain straw base in two colors of ribbon makes a simple base to contrast a dramatic bouquet of evergreens.

The fresh beauty of evergreens can be preserved by standing them in a solution of three parts warm water to one part glycerin for about two weeks, or until their color begins to change. Keep them in a warm place and replenish any liquid that evaporates with more of the water/glycerin solution. (Several small slices in the stem will ensure good glycerin absorption.) Although they'll lose their deep green color, these treated branches are extremely durable and will last almost indefinitely.

A plain 14-inch (36-cm.) straw base wrapped with red velvet and green satin ribbons makes a subtle backdrop for a bouquet of fresh hemlock and pine cones. The greenery was picked on 3-inch (8-cm.) wooden picks and inserted into the base, while the cones were wired and picked. The ribbon was added last with a long floral pin.

Evergreen Wreaths

Only evergreen wreaths echo the medieval traditions of swags and garlands, of bringing greenery indoors during cold winter months. Of course these wreaths make great Christmas decorations when interspersed with red or silver, as we so frequently see today, but their beauty and scent should be enjoyed throughout the year. If you're a city dweller and finding fresh evergreen branches proves to be a problem, check with local florists who often keep them in stock during the holiday season for their own arrangements.

The medley of evergreens to the right adds an interesting variety of color and texture to the wreath. The wreath began by outlining a 14-inch (36-cm.) straw base with fresh boxwood that was attached with pins. Clumps of fir, hemlock, arbor vitae, and cedar were picked in, and then more boxwood was added for depth. The bow was outlined with holly after it was wired on, and then artificial berries were glued to the holly. (Real holly berries tend to fall off easily and are dangerous if you have young children around.)

Evergreens galore! Clumps of hemlock, fir, arbor vitae, and cedar were attached to a straw base with floral picks. Bright red holly berries were added for color.

The bells in this dynamic wreath are sure to put anyone in a festive mood. Nine feet of silk pine garland attached to a 16-inch (41-cm.) straw base with greening pins got this wreath off to a quick start. The wicker bells, bows, and clusters of silk fruit were attached to the base with greening pins and wooden picks. After the bows were pinned on, clusters of dried sugar bush and German statice were added.

Cinnamon and cones complement a garland of pine evergreens in the wreath to the right. The garland was attached to a wire ring with floral wire and sprigs of frosted pine were hot glued on to give the wreath a fuller look. A small piece of foam covered with Spanish moss glued to the base serves as an anchor for the cinnamon sticks, pine cone branches, and ribbon. (The cinnamon sticks are available in bulk at specialty food stores, particularly those selling Indian spices.)

Miniature bouquets of bells, silk fruit, sugar bush, and German statice were attached to a straw base covered with silk pine.

A plaid ribbon meanders through a wreath of pine garland, cinnamon sticks, pine branches, and cones. Some of the branches were highlighted with spray frost.

Dried Flowers

Although nothing can really parallel the beauty of fresh-cut flowers, mankind certainly made one of his greatest compromises with nature when he learned to dry flowers. Color, texture, shape, and even iridescence can be preserved in the drying process, and what better showcase for this beauty than a wreath?

Certain flowers — annual statice, bachelor buttons and strawflowers, for example — can be found in almost every possible color, ranging from soft hues to sharp, vibrant shades. This wide color range enables the designer to customize a wreath for a particular room or location. And since the flowers are inserted into the base with floral picks, they can easily be removed and new colors added if you decide to re-decorate or want to display the wreath in a new location. Many dried flowers also offer the added bonus of retaining their fragrances, and will pleasantly perfume the air around them.

When choosing your wreath materials, keep in mind the wide variety of dried grasses and seed pods that are also available. In most cases you'll find they provide a wonderful color and texture contrast to the stark beauty of dried flowers. Another way to complement a wreath of dried flowers is to add some light, wispy materials such as caspia or German statice.

Reminiscent of the aura of 19th-century dried flower wreaths, this dramatic melange of large and small dried flowers was surprisingly quick to make. A commercially available 30-inch (76-cm.) silk pine wreath served as the base, and the dried materials were attached with hot glue. The wreath's outline was established first with larkspur and eucalyptus. Heavier materials were added next and the filler material last. The dried flowers and foliage included: protea, cockscomb, yarrow, amaranthus, statice. The streamers that meander through the wreath and the bow were wired onto the base.

The rising popularity of dried flowers has encouraged many retail stores and mail order companies to stock a wide variety of dried materials, although you may still want to grow your own. Surprisingly, many people — even those with wonderful spring and summer gardens — avoid drying their own flowers because they assume it's too complicated. Actually, the most

A dramatic melange of large dried flowers embedded in an assortment of evergreens. This 34-inch (86-cm.) wreath is reminiscent of 19th century dried flower wreaths. Note the ribbon meandering through the wreath.

difficult part of drying flowers is finding a warm, dry place to keep the flowers during the drying process.

The most popular method of drying flowers is to hang them, upside down, from the ceiling. The process is simple, and works well for almost every sturdy-stemmed plant. The stems are grouped in small clusters, and then tied together with string. The amount of time required to completely dry your flowers will vary, depending on the type of flower and the amount of moisture in your drying area (plan on at least several weeks), so be sure to check on them every few days.

For flowers with more delicate heads, a drying rack or a moisture-absorbing substance may yield better results. You can make your own drying rack by stretching fine chicken wire or window screening over a wooden frame. The stems are then dropped through the holes so the flower heads rest on the wire or mesh.

The commercially available drying substances such as silica gel often do a better job of preserving the color of some delicate flowers. In this method, the flowers are placed in a box or canister and the drying substance is poured over them like sand, until they're completely covered. Plants dried in this way tend to re-

Dried Flowers

absorb moisture and will wilt, so if you live in a humid environment or plan to hang your wreath in a moist place, such as the kitchen or bathroom, choose another method.

"Tis a gift to be simple" aptly applies to the wreath above left made solely of German statice. Its delicate statement of elegance would enhance any room. If you grow bored with the wreath or want to perk it up for a holiday or a party, add a few clusters of colorful dried flowers for a quick change in design. The statice was tied in bunches and inserted with wire into an 18-inch (46-cm.) straw base.

Small clusters of German statice were wired onto an 18-inch (46-cm.) double-tiered metal ring to form a base for the wreath below. Branches of heather were then blended into the statice to give the wreath its lavender color, and trios of rosy-red strawflowers were added last. One fun aspect of this wreath is how easily the color scheme can be changed by removing and adding flowers.

The fragrant green and gold wreath to the right started with a 14-inch (36-cm.) straw base that was wrapped in clear plastic for extra support. Small clusters of eucalyptus were wired to a wooden pick and then attached to the base from the outside inward, with care given to keeping all the material slanting in the same direction. Baby's breath and dried cotton husks make the perfect complements.

Above: An 18-inch (46-cm.) simple wreath of only German statice tied in bunches and inserted in the straw base.

Below: An 18-inch (46-cm.) wreath made from German statice, dried straw flowers, and heather. A double-tiered metal base was used.

TIPS FOR GOOD DRYING RESULTS

1. Timing is everything when it comes to harvesting flowers for drying. Experiment with picking plants at all stages of their blooming cycle. (Some flowers work best when picked as buds, while others need their buds fully opened.)
2. Avoid picking flowers during extreme heat, when their blooms tend to droop; or when their blossoms are wet, after a rainstorm or a foggy morning, for example.
3. Store unused, dried flowers in boxes in a moisture-free environment.
4. Always dry substantially more material than you'll need. The finished product is fragile and breaks easily.
5. Check all flowers carefully before picking. Insect bites and discolorations increase (not decrease) in the finished product.
6. Check your drying flowers often (about every three days) to prevent overdrying. (Flowers that are too dry will fall apart.)

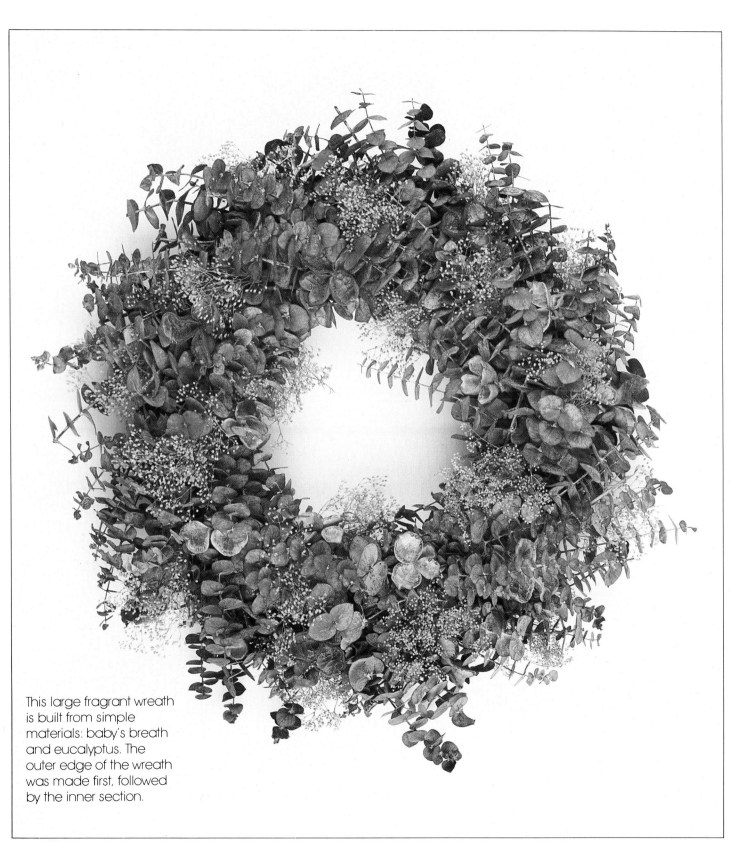

This large fragrant wreath is built from simple materials: baby's breath and eucalyptus. The outer edge of the wreath was made first, followed by the inner section.

A moss base was the start of this Victorian-style wreath.

Dried Flowers

The medley of bright flowers shown left echoes the Victorian traditions of wreathmaking. An 11-inch (28-cm.) moss base was covered with German statice. Yarrow, cockscomb, statice, roses, astilbe, feverfew, lamb's ear, rose leaves, strawflower, and baby's breath were then arranged and glued. To give the wreath its exuberant character, several light wisps of caspia were added. The final touch was a Victorian-style lace and ribbon bow.

A bridal bouquet becomes a cherished heirloom when made into a wreath. Shown above, a 10-inch (25-cm.) moss base was adorned first with baby's breath attached with hot glue. Then roses from the bride's bouquet were glue-gunned on, with the white ribbons added last. This wreath would make a wonderful memento for any bride, or a special gift for her bridesmaids or attendants when their bouquets are preserved.

A 14-inch (36-cm.) vine base wrapped with Spanish moss, below, was the start of this delicate bouquet of roses, German statice, and baby's breath. The statice was attached first with a glue gun to form a background. Then the roses and baby's breath were arranged and wired onto the base.

Roses and ribbon from a bride's bouquet were transformed into a lasting keepsake.

Right, curling tendrils of ribbon meander through a bouquet of roses, German statice, and baby's breath.

A collection of wild-flowers and grasses in hues of yellow, silver, and brown gives the wreath, at left, the qualities of warmth and sunshine of an autumn day. The wreath started with a 16-inch (41-cm.) moss base, into which yellow yarrow, goldenrod, iron weed, white yarrow, golden marguerite, bee balm, grasses, black-eyed Susan, and clematis were inserted with floral picks.

The delicate blooms of dried flowers, herbs, seed heads, and grasses, right, were steel-picked into a 14-inch (36-cm.) straw base for a stunning effect. Rose hip, roses, wild mint, mountain mint, santolina, Queen Anne's lace, echinacea, bee balm, goldenrod, white and pink yarrow, and amaranth were picked onto the base, while an assortment of dried grasses outline the inner and outer edges of the base. In addition to being beautiful, the wreath's herbs also emit a delicate perfume.

A study of autumn colors with yellow yarrow, goldenrod, ironweed, white yarrow, golden marguerite, bee balm, grasses, black-eyed Susan, and clematis.

Seed heads, herbs, and
grasses are blended with
dried flowers for a
wreath that's fragrant
and beautiful.

A wide variety of crisp silver and white dried flowers imparts a wonderful sense of texture to the wreath shown here. The inside ring was established with wispy clumps of German statice, attached to an 18-inch (46-cm.) straw base with floral picks. Baby's breath, strawflower, acroclinium, salvia, pearly everlasting, gomphrena, celosia, and lamb's ear make up the rest of the wreath. Note that larger clusters of flowers can be handsome when surrounded by delicate sprays of other varieties.

Celosia, pearly everlasting, salvia, and statice provided the vibrant colors for the patriotic celebration of red, white, and blue shown right above. The inner edge of a 16-inch (41-cm.) straw base was floral-picked first with celosia; then the outer edge was outlined with white and blue salvia. Because special care was given to the flowers during the harvesting and drying process, their colors will stay bright for years to come.

An assortment of flowers and mosses gives the wreath, below right, the texture and color of a living flower garden. The wreath started with an 8-inch (20-cm.) moss base that was then covered with sheet moss (purchased from a florist wholesaler) using pins. This gives the wreath its full, rounded

shape. The flowers were wired onto the base in random order, and then glue-gunned for reinforcement. The wreath is quick to make, and would certainly be a welcome gift for those who miss their flower gardens during the snow season.

German statice outlines the inner and outer rings, while baby's breath, strawflower, acroclinium, salvia, pearly everlasting, gomphrena, celosia, and lamb's ear fill in the middle.

FLOWER COLORS

Finding flowers with beautiful color is never a problem; finding flowers that hold their beautiful color after drying often is. Following are examples of flowers that dry well, retain their color, and are generally easy to find through retail markets.

Silver
lamb's ear
honesty
silver king artemisia
xeranthemum
melaeuca
daisy bush
stirlingia

White and Cream
pearly everlasting
yarrow
baby's breath
German statice
cotton
astilbe
lamb's tongue

Purple and Blue
delphinium
strawflower
lavender
astilbe
statice
cornflower
globe thistle

Green and Brown
pin oak
hydrangea
love-in-a-mist
bee balm
dill
bamboo
ivy

Orange and Yellow
pot marigold
santolina
statice
strawflower
goldenrod
tansy
yarrow

Red and Pink
sunray
rose hip
celosia
Russian statice
yarrow
campion
globe amaranth

A patriotic (red, white, and blue) wreath featuring blue and white salvias, pearly everlasting, red celosia, and blue and white statice sinuata.

A small 8-inch (20-cm.) moss base was covered with sheet moss for extra fullness. Bright flowers were then wired on.

CONSERVATION

If you're feeling adventurous and decide to go on a flower-gathering expedition for drying materials, do make a quick phone call to your local library or conservation club for a list of endangered plants. (Because this endangered list varies from area to area, you may find that some of the materials used in this book are endangered in your area. Rest assured: our picking activities were both legal and moral.)

Garden clubs are also a great source for the horticulture novice. Ask for advice on gathering locations, plants that dry well and retain their color, etc. It's also a good idea to investigate any laws your area might have on picking wildflowers, and to familiarize yourself with local poisonous plants.

A traditional holiday wreath
is both decorative and
meaningful when made
of symbolic flowers
and foliage.

Floral Messages

When a close family member or friend celebrates a special occasion, it's often difficult to come up with an equally special gift; hunting through a department store for some mass-produced gift just doesn't seem appropriate, and the messages on greeting cards never seem specific or sincere enough. Somehow, we want to tell someone just how we feel, and to make it intimately personal and remembered.

The wreaths in this chapter take advantage of the historical meanings of flowers, meanings that have been passed down through history, often coming from rural folk legends and traditions. Medieval and Renaissance paintings frequently featured bouquets of flowers in the background which imparted symbolic meaning to either the painting itself or to the painter.

Based on the chart, you can create your own personal message by making a wreath. Consider making a wreath for an anniversary, wedding, new home, birth, graduation, a new job, or retirement — or celebrate something very personal in someone's life — the planting of a new garden, the ending of a smoking habit, a special friend moving away, or a heartfelt condolence to a bereaved friend.

Along with the gift wreath, enclose a card describing the plants used and their meanings. There is no doubt that the gift will be appreciated and shared with others for many seasons to come.

Many plants and herbs also have special meanings in religious history. The advent wreath shown here celebrates the four weeks preceeding Christmas and is made from herbs rich in religious symbolism. The following herbs were picked into a 14-inch (36-cm.) straw base: bay leaves (glory and eternal life); sage (timelessness); rosemary (the Blessed Virgin); sweet myrtle (the Messiah's promises); mountain mint (eternal refreshment); thyme (the manger); lavender (virtue); rue (repentance). Tansy, white yarrow, and rose hips were added for color. With a quick investigation into your own religious history, your holiday wreaths can be transformed into more than just decoration.

COMMON PLANT & FLOWER MEANINGS

Amaranth	immortality	Mints	eternal refreshment
Balm	sympathy	Mistletoe	love
Basil	good wishes	Moss	maternal love
Bay	glory	Oregano	substance
Bittersweet	harmony	Parsley	festivity
Bluebell	constancy	Pine	humility
Chives	usefulness	Rose	love
Clematis	mental beauty	Rosemary	remembrance
Cockscomb	affectation	Rue	grace, clear vision
Coriander	hidden worth	Sage	wisdom, immortality
Cumin	fidelity	Salvia, blue	I think of you
Fennel	flattery	Salvia, red	forever mine
Fern	sincerity	Spruce	stateliness
Holly	hope, divinity	Sunflower	false riches
Honesty	wealth	Tansy	hostile thoughts
Horehound	health	Tarragon	lasting interest
Ivy	God, friendship	Thyme	courage, strength
Larkspur	lightness	Wormwood	absence
Lavender	devotion	Yarrow	war
Marigold	uneasiness		

Many plants and herbs have biblical meanings which may or may not correspond to their secular meanings.

Carnation	first love	Magnolia	pride, power
Chrysanthemum	long life	Oak	forgiveness, eternity
Crape Myrtle	longlasting	Olive branch	peace
Daisy	innocence	Palm	eternal peace
Dianthus	divine love	Peach blossom	long life
Evergreens	life everlasting	Plum	longevity
Gardenia	femininity	Poinsettia	fertility, eternity
Gladiolus	Incarnation	Shamrock	Holy Trinity
Gourd	resurrection	Thistle	man's fall
Hyacinth	prudence	Thorn	grief
Ivy	eternity, fidelity	Violet	humility
Laurel	triumph, eternity	Wheat	staff of life
Madonna Lily	resurrection		

The wreath shown left celebrates a child's birth with the following plants picked into a 7-inch (18-cm.) straw base: elshaltzia (sweetness); celandine (joys to come); clover-white (think of me); coreopsis (always cheerful); mallow (mildness); mint (virtue); myrtle (love); sorrel (affection); verbena (pure and guileless). The background was made of German statice, baby's breath, white salvia, and pearly everlasting.

Welcome a new child with a special birth wreath. The wreath is still beautiful after it dries and makes a nice keepsake.

Messages

The wedding wreath at right started with a 10-inch (25-cm.) straw base. The following plants were picked into a background of German statice: dogwood (durability); amaranth (unfading love); bay leaf (I change but in death); celandine (joys to come); fern (sincerity); goat's rue (reason); heath (solitude); myrtle (love); ivy (fidelity); sage (domestic virtue); salvia-blue (I think of you).

Give the newlyweds a unique gift filled with special meaning. Again, the wreath dries nicely.

Herbal Wreaths

There is something hauntingly mysterious and elusive about an herbal wreath. Perhaps because herbs have such a long history of culinary, medicinal, aromatic, and symbolic uses. To investigate these historic uses and meanings makes for fascinating reading: it's as if some medieval or Biblical relic is growing in our time, on our land.

Modern medicine was born through studying the effects of various herbs on the human body. We still take horehound drops with a sore throat, and are rediscovering the effects of various teas. The culinary uses of herbs are also being rediscovered, as is the joy of growing herbs for their beauty and usefulness. And, of course, one must not forget the smells of herbs, filling the air with sweetness, pungency, mystery, and joy.

The wreaths here were designed by Kate Jayne of the Sandy Mush Herbal Nursery. Her immediate and extended family have devoted their entire lives to growing and finding new ways to enjoy the almost limitless number of herbs.

While Kate raises all her own herbs for her herbal wreaths, you too can find, locally or through the mails, herbs of every variety. They can also be found in health food stores, at herbal pharmacies (they still exist, you just have to look), and don't forget to ask local gardening groups — there's bound to be an herbalist or two in any group of size.

Kate starts with a home-made straw base which she makes, oddly enough, from straw and spool wire. (For directions, see page 30.) The dried herbs are then put in small bunches of three to five stems, each made from one to three different herbs. The stem is snipped to 1½ to 3 inches (4 to 8 cm.) and put onto picks. (Any leaves on the bottom portion of the stem have been removed.) Wreaths such as those pictured take 30 to 60 picks.

HERBS FOR WREATHS

Below is a partial list of herbs that can be used in wreaths. They can be purchased from herb growers through the mail or grown at home. Besides being useful in wreaths, they also have other properties that make them attractive.

Common Name	Lifecycle	Properties
Ambrosia	annual	fragrant
Artemisia, silver	perennial	
Feverfew	perennial	insect repellant, fragrant
Garlic	perennial	culinary, medicinal
Horehound	perennial	candy
Lambs Ear	perennial	
Lavender (English)	perennial	potpourri, medicinal
Mints	perennial	culinary, fragrant
Sages	varies	culinary, fragrant
Rue	perennial	insect repellant
Southernwood	perennial	insect repellant, fragrant
Wormwoods	varies	fragrant
Yarrow	perennial	

A **tour de force** in herbal wreaths, with a few cheats for color: statice latifolia, oak leaf, hydrangea, margaritacea, German statice, annual statice, Queen Anne's lace, rose, stantolina, pearly everlasting, veronica, astilbe, strawflower, feverfew, daffodil, and coreopsis.

Herbal

A study in golds, silvers, and pinks made from rose, Queen Anne's lace, artemisia, yellow yarrow, white yarrow, lamb's ear, feverfew, oak leaf hydrangea, astilbe, catnip, lucida stellata, and, as a final touch of red, a peony.

The soft hues of lamb's ear, artemesia, clover, salvia, gomphrena, lavender, pink yarrow, German statice, self-heal, chive blossoms, and acroclinium were steel-picked onto a straw base.

Culinary Wreaths

Those of you who enjoy a special relationship with your kitchen are in for a real treat. By now we hope you realize that wreaths can be made from almost anything, and the kitchen is a great place to find ingredients. Once finished, these wreaths easily become an intrinsic part of your kitchen's decor (an herb wreath, for example, looks great over the spice rack), so keep this in mind when you start.

Some of the culinary wreaths shown in this chapter are great for adventurous cooks. Just hang them near your stove and remove ingredients as you need them. The wreaths can be redesigned every few weeks by adding new spices and herbs to fill in the bare spots. Even if you don't use them often, they'll make welcome aromatic additions to your home.

For a vegetable wreath that will never spoil, a 14-inch (36-cm.) purchased straw base was outlined with green burlap ribbon to establish an attractive base. Loops of raffia were pinned around the paper and then silk vegetables from a crafts supply shop were glued to the base. The vegetables with flat edges — carrots and celery, for example — were laid in first, followed by the round items. Looped ribbon streamers and tree ferns were worked in to soften the edges.

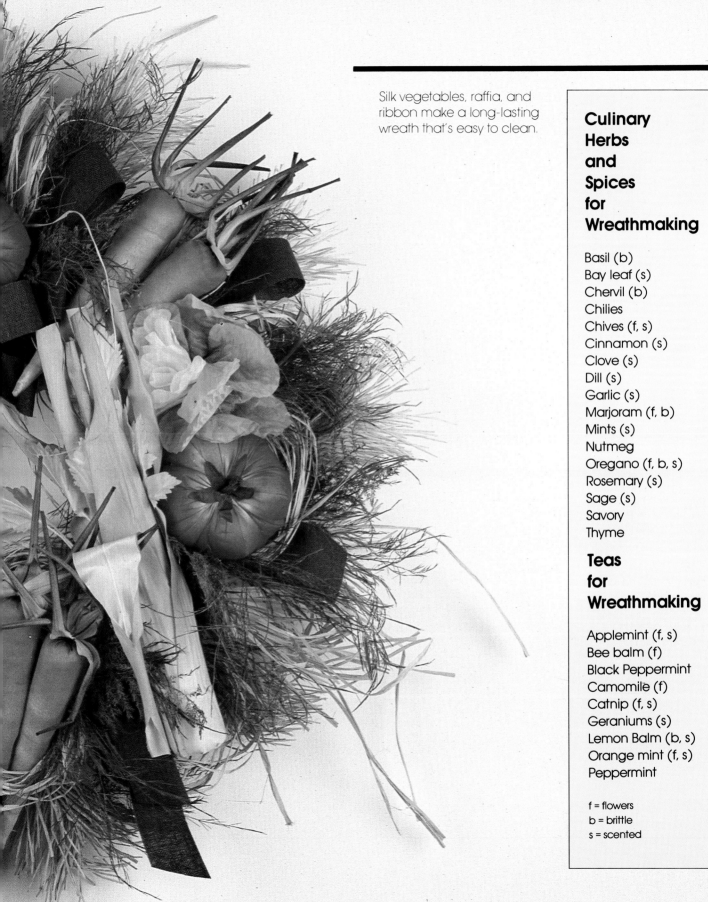

Silk vegetables, raffia, and ribbon make a long-lasting wreath that's easy to clean.

Culinary Herbs and Spices for Wreathmaking

Basil (b)
Bay leaf (s)
Chervil (b)
Chilies
Chives (f, s)
Cinnamon (s)
Clove (s)
Dill (s)
Garlic (s)
Marjoram (f, b)
Mints (s)
Nutmeg
Oregano (f, b, s)
Rosemary (s)
Sage (s)
Savory
Thyme

Teas for Wreathmaking

Applemint (f, s)
Bee balm (f)
Black Peppermint
Camomile (f)
Catnip (f, s)
Geraniums (s)
Lemon Balm (b, s)
Orange mint (f, s)
Peppermint

f = flowers
b = brittle
s = scented

Culinary Wreaths

A medley of culinary delights, left, generates a quick source for cooking ingredients and a fragrant aroma. The inner and outer circles of a 16-inch (41-cm.) straw base were outlined first with clumps of bay leaves. Then clumps of sage leaves, garlic bulbs, red peppers, and blooms of safflower, mint, lavender, bee balm, and anise hyssop.

The garlic wreath at right started with a 16-inch (41-cm.) straw base to which whole garlic cloves were picked in and then hot-glued for reinforcement. Oregano, chive heads, hot peppers, and sage were glued on and make the wreath a colorful reservoir of cooking ingredients.

Left, clumps of bay leaves outline the inner and outer circles of a 16-inch (41-cm.) straw base, while dried flowers and herbs add a medley of color and fragrance.

Right, garlic cloves, oregano, chive heads, hot peppers, and sage make this wreath into a hanging spice rack.

This fragrant wreath of solid bay leaves will leave your soups and sauces always well seasoned.

The traditional bay leaf makes an elegant wreath all by itself, or use it as a backdrop for other herbs and spices. The wreath shown here uses bay leaves purchased in bulk from an herbal nursery with the leaves still on the branches. They're easier to work with and less expensive this way, but if you can only find single bay leaves at a specialty shop or restaurant, they can be gathered together in small numbers and attached with glue. Or, if they have stems, they can be picked into the wreath.

Instead of peeling the potatoes, why not put them in a wreath? Small clumps of moss were tucked into the crevices to prevent the styrofoam base from showing.

Small red potatoes and moss make a quick, fun, and attractive wreath. The potatoes were inserted into a 9-inch (23-cm.) styrofoam base with wooden picks and then hot-glued for reinforcement. Moss was then tucked into the crevices to give the wreath shape and color. Other vegetables, such as garlic, onions, green onions or sweet potatoes can be substituted or added, but do keep the format small since these wreaths are quite heavy. Eventually the vegetables will spoil, but that only gives you an excuse to make another wreath!

Left, a collection of wine corks was creatively arranged and glued to a straw base, with dried flowers and moss added as embellishment.

When looking for kitchen wreath ingredients, don't overlook the non-edibles. If you like entertaining with wine, let guests sign and date each wine cork as it's popped for a special occasion. After you've collected a number of corks, insert them into a straw or ribbon-wrapped base with wooden picks (experiment with placement for the best effect) and then hot glue them for reinforcement. In our wreath we tucked Spanish moss into the bare spots and added dried flowers. (We used golden yarrow, caspia, and excelsior, but other dried flowers would work just as well.) This wreath would hang nicely over the wine rack or bar area. If you're intrigued with this wreath but don't want to invest in a case of wine, ask a local restaurant to save the corks for you in return for a wreath you make for them.

A collection of kitchen utensils, cinnamon sticks, and artificial berries form an interesting montage to the right. A 12-inch (30-cm.) styrofoam base was wrapped in ribbon and then secured with a glue gun. To keep the wreath low-cost, look for utensils in second-hand stores, clean out a few kitchen drawers, or check with friends. Some fun alternatives would be using all wooden or plastic utensils, or using a collection of measuring spoons, whisks, or tea strainers.

Right, cinnamon sticks, artificial berries, and a variety of utensils from the kitchen drawer were glue-gunned to a small styrofoam base.

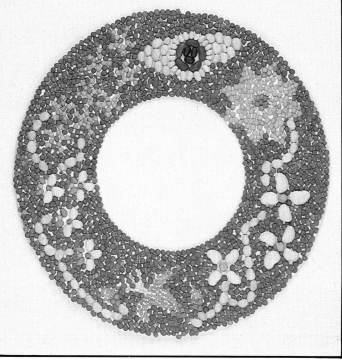

If you've traditionally decorated your Christmas tree with strung popcorn, here's a great way to keep it in use after the tree comes down. (Of course, you'll have to unstring it.) The popcorn was hot-glued onto a 10-inch (25-cm.) styrofoam base. (Hint: stale popcorn glues more easily.) Then berry sprays made of silk were arranged and glued, with small green apples, twigs, and ribbon pinned on next. The wreath won't last indefinitely, but a thin layer of sprayed shellac will preserve it longer.

A 10-inch (25-cm.) styro-foam base was covered with popped corn, silk berries, green apples, twigs, and ribbon.

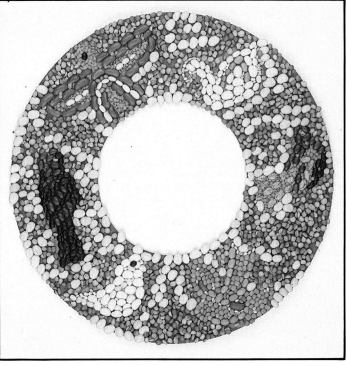

A sheet of framing matte board cut to a 14-inch (36-cm.) diameter makes a clever base for these wreaths made with dried beans. Bird and flower designs were first sketched onto the board. Then an assortment of colored beans — green and yellow split peas, lima beans, and kidney beans — were white-glued in place. The design areas were filled in first, and then the back-ground. School children could easily design their own wreaths by tracing one of their favorite pictures from a coloring book or cartoon onto the wreath base. Following the same format, a collection of buttons or other small items could easily be converted into a wreath.

A bean wreath makes an absorbing children's pro-ject for a rainy day. The base was made from a piece of framing matte board.

The braided wreath to the left looks good enough to eat — and after the photo shoot we did just that. The bread is delicious, sweet and firm. (See page 140 for recipe.) Brush the wreath with melted butter before and during baking for an extra sheen. This wreath would be great for a holiday get-together, Christmas dinner, or as a festive gift. If you choose not to eat the wreath, it can be preserved by spraying on a coat of matte polyurethane.

A wreath of fresh fruit makes a wonderful table centerpiece for a party, or it can be placed right on the buffet table as part of the menu. The fruit wreath to the right started with a 16-inch (41-cm.) styrofoam base that was covered with sheet moss using hot glue. The red and green apples were attached with wooden picks, as were the ornamental pineapples. The black grapes were attached with U-shaped wire pins. (Note: If you plan to hang this wreath on a wall, the elements should be hot-glued after they're picked in for reinforcement.) For a party with a more tropical theme, try using lemons, oranges, bananas, and kiwi.

A Challah bread recipe is mixed, allowed to rise, and then braided into the wreath shape. The wreath can be eaten or preserved with shellac.

Transform the contents of
the traditional fruit bowl
into a quick wreath with
wooden picks, hot glue,
and a styrofoam base.

Wreath Tableaux

It is not always necessary to cover the entire wreath base. If you love browsing in knick-knack shops but hesitate to make purchases because you don't know what you'd do with them once you get home, keep in mind that even the simplest base becomes an under-stated and sophisticated backdrop for dramatic additions. Here are three examples of elegant wreaths made by allowing the base to work as an integral part of the wreath

The triple wreath creates a warm spring feeling in the midst of a gloomy winter. After three 8-inch (20-cm.) twig wreaths were wired and glued together, the three bows were added. Then birds and silk berry sprigs were added, with a final touch of caspia. (The caspia is added last because it's so

Three wreaths are the charm. The wreaths are wired together and finished off with three bows, a bevy of birds, and a touch of caspia.

delicate.) This same wreath could easily have been decorated with some silver ornaments and sprays of pine to make a unique Christmas wreath.

In the next wreath, Spanish moss was tucked into a 22-inch (56-cm.) grapevine base. "American Prestige" silk roses were then glued to the base, after which sarracenia lilies (also called swamp lily or pitcher plant) were glued in. (The sarracenia were bought fresh and then dried. For drying instructions, see page 73.) Last, dabs of moss were added to create a wreath that would look handsome above the mantel or in a bedroom.

The enchanting wreath opposite was once a store-bought 12-inch (30-cm.) straw wreath that was covered with moss using pins. The large bow was added next, and then the dramatic final touch of a bird nesting in moss on a pussy willow branch. We found this particular bird in a craft store, but if you're not happy with their selections, try pilfering through Christmas ornaments.

Simple drama is created with silk roses, naturally dried sarracenia lilies, and Spanish moss around a simple grapevine base.

A single bird awaits spring from her perch in a grove of pussy willows. This scenic wreath starts by pinning moss to a small straw wreath.

Living Wreaths

Fresh flower and greenery clippings from the garden were placed into water-filled test tubes and then inserted into a base.

For plant and horticulture enthusiasts, a living wreath is the perfect challenge of patience and skill. Beyond the challenge, these living wreaths offer a lushness in color and texture that's unmatched by even the most sophisticated plastic and silk fakes. A living wreath can be nurtured and shaped to become a traditional wall wreath; or, with a little forethought, they can be grown around a punchbowl, candle, or other centerpiece.

A basic "how-to" for creating live wreaths doesn't exist. The four living wreaths in this chapter were each made a different way, and countless other methods exist. Any tool-of-the-trade that works in your garden can work for your living wreath, or spend an afternoon at a florist's shop to investigate his trade secrets. Experimentation and a loving touch will yield the best results.

This wreath of fresh flowers makes an innovative replacement for the traditional vase. The wreath started with a 16-inch (41-cm.) grapevine base, into which stems of glycerin-preserved evergreens were inserted. The flowers were inserted into the base in individual water-filled test tubes (available from a floral shop) and can be changed as often as you like. The bow was attached to the base with wire.

Another treasure available through florists is a pre-made oasis ring form, which gives the wreath its circular shape and at the same time allows the living material to stay fresh in a water base. For the wreath to the right, English ivy, galax leaves, prince's pine, and hydrangea were inserted into the oasis ring. The wreath is quick to make and can easily be freshened with a light misting of water.

A water-filled base keeps a wreath of English ivy, prince's pine, and hydrangea looking fresh and green.

The creeping nature of a rosemary plant, left, was lured into a wreath shape by a diligent plant lover. The wreath's base was made of a heavy metal wire spraypainted green to keep it unobtrusive. To encourage the plant to grow in one direction, it was sometimes necessary to tie it to the base with raffia. The rosemary plant is tolerant of indoor living, blooms almost year-round, and emits a wonderful fragrance. If you grow bored with the gold fabric or want to create a new seasonal look, just tuck a new piece of fabric around the pot.

A rosemary bush was tenderly tamed into a wreath shape, and needs only regular clipping and watering to maintain its beauty.

The base for this wreath of live succulents, below, was made from chicken wire, sheet moss, and potting soil. The wire was first shaped into an open circle, with a thick layer of sheet moss lining the circle's bottom. A thick layer of potting soil was then packed on top of the moss, and the entire base was given a light misting of water. The plants were planted in the dirt and secured through the chicken wire with metal U-shaped pins. To finish the wreath, another layer of moss was tucked around the plants to completely cover the dirt. With a burning candle in the middle, this wreath would make a gorgeous table centerpiece. (Just be sure to place it on a large plate or sheet of plastic to prevent water damage.) Another way to use the wire, moss and dirt base is to insert fresh clippings into the base and allow them to take root in the moss.

Moss and potting soil were inserted into a base of chicken wire to form a living wreath garden.

Table Wreaths

Where is it written that a wreath must hang on the wall? Creative hosts/hostesses have long used wreaths as distinctive centerpieces. Table wreaths take no more work than wall wreaths, and allow the addition of materials that would be inappropriate for hanging wreaths. While other wreaths in this book would be equally at home on a table, here are several wreaths that were designed specifically for gracing a dining room or coffee table, or a library table in a den.

For drama and beauty, few wreaths can compete with a composition of fresh and dried flowers. They're both a centerpiece and a conversation piece for any gala spring or summer dinner party.

The wreath itself was made from a vine base with an assortment of picked dried materials, including globe amaranth, roses, white statice, mushrooms, and moss. The fresh ingredients include lilies, galax and chrysanthemums. The fresh elements will last several days because they were inserted into the wreath in small, elongated tubes of water which are frequently used by, and available from, floral shops. A slight misting before the party will freshen the live materials, which can be easily removed and the base reused.

A truly elegant and colorful combination of dried and fresh flowers on a vine base will glorify any dining table. It's deceptively easy to make as well.

Perhaps a quiet corner would be the proper home for this idyllic scene. A blue loon sits on a pad of sponge mushrooms in front of a twig wreath while painted reeds ascend upward.

The wreath to the left is a contemplative composition centered around a small, painted model of a blue loon. A small piece of styrofoam was glued underneath the loon, onto which dried mushrooms were then glued to create his perch. The dried materials — reeds, feathers, and a spray of berries — were arranged and then glue-gunned onto the base. Moss was added to fill in the gaps.

The wreath to the right is almost oriental in feeling. Strong vertical elements of bamboo twigs and seed pods are balanced with the arrangement of dried sponge mushrooms, dried flowers, and the exposed wreath base of grasses. The elements are all glue-gunned (the bamboo twigs are inserted into the base first). The beauty of this wreath is partially the result of very basic, unadorned materials simply used.

This artistic composition is made from a simple assortment of unadorned materials, creating a still, quiet table wreath.

Table Wreaths

A celebration of the harvest brings these autumnal elements together in a simple yet festive wreath, fashioned from fresh grapes and berries balanced with dried materials.

For fall and winter, what could be more appropriate than a wreath that celebrates the fruits of the harvest: fresh grapes and berries, nuts, pumpkins, gourds, Indian corn, red chilies and, for a bit of humor, small red potatoes. The clumps of grapes should be inserted into the vine base on the day of the wreath's use and the berries placed on the grapes. The potatoes are put on the base with hidden toothpicks. Again, the basic wreath arrangement can be retained for many years, with appropriate fresh ingredients added with each use.

Your guests at a cocktail reception or formal dinner will never forget your fantastic hors d'oeuvres wreath made with shrimp, cherry tomatoes, radishes, marinated mushrooms, and snow peas. All the elements are inserted with toothpicks on a ribbon-wrapped foam base. The candles are pushed into the base and held in place with glue. (Warning: don't place food at the base of the candle — wax drippings don't taste good.) Final flourishes include a few galax leaves, parsley, loops of ribbon pinned to the base and a hearty sprig of pyracantha.

The edible wreath idea could also have been made with fresh fruits, colorful cheeses or, for a decadent alternative, chocolates. The possibilities are deliciously endless.

Any cocktail reception or buffet dinner is rendered instantly memorable with this colorful 16-inch (41-cm.) delicious wreath. It's as simple to make as it is pleasant to eat. For even more drama, place the wreath on an iced silver tray.

Wreath napkin holders make any table seem festive. Use them for special family dinners, or give them away as mementos after a gala dinner party. They only take a few minutes to make with fresh vines or twigs.

Here's a quick, cheerful addition to any table: small 3-inch (8-cm.) napkin holders made by intertwining short lengths of vines and decorated with small, glued strawflowers and a simple tied bit of ribbon. For a special occasion, invite the guests to take home their wreath as a souvenir of the occasion.

The wreath ensemble below doesn't need to be saved for a special occasion. The larger wreath was made from a straw base, picked with German statice and an assortment of dried strawflowers. The smaller wreaths were constructed from quickly made vine wreaths, and were also picked with a few sprigs of German statice and strawflowers. The candles are held in place with a bit of modeling clay. For more formal occasions, consider making similar small wreaths to hold place cards.

A simple arrangement of dried flowers and colorful candles makes an elegant centerpiece, drawing attention with its warmth and color. A simple change of candle color and the trio gains a new personality.

Scented Wreaths

Scented wreaths add a whole new realm of possibilities to wreath design and function. Coincidentally, most items that emit a pleasant fragrance — cinnamon and potpourri, for example — look beautiful in wreaths. And, once you've created a great-smelling wreath, we hope you'll consider hanging it somewhere out of the ordinary. Kitchens and bathrooms make ideal homes for scented wreaths. (Their moist, warm atmospheres encourage the release of the wreath's scents.)

Bags of potpourri added to an ordinary wreath make it a great addition to a linen or clothing closet; or consider spraying your favorite scent directly onto a wreath — the dried materials will absorb the scent and gradually release it over time. Keep in mind that most of the scented materials found in department stores at such high prices are available in bulk from craft stores or specialty food shops at considerable savings.

A pound of cinnamon sticks and clumps of preserved fraser fir make an enchanting fragrance combination. (See page 68 for greenery preservation techniques.) The cinnamon was glued onto a 12-inch (30-cm.) base, with the longer sticks radiating out from the center. The spaces were filled in with fraser fir, and small pieces of cinnamon added on top. The wreath was finished by wiring a bow around the base.

Lower left is a unique wreath that works time-and-a-half. While attractive to look at, the wreath's ingredients tend to repel moths, making it ideal for closets and basements. Nicotiana (tobacco) was white-glued to a straw base, with sandalwood, whole cloves, and hawthorne berry added on with a glue gun.

The bathroom wreath shown right started with a 16-inch (41-cm.) vine base, to which small bags of potpourri were attached with multi-colored satin ribbon. Clumps of wild grapes, celosia, straw-flower, gomphrena, pearly everlasting, statice, pomanders, and yellow yarrow were attached next with ribbon, raffia, or string.

Top, cinnamon sticks and fraser fir emit wonderful fragrances.

Left, nicotiana, sandalwood, and berries make a charming wreath for damp, musty rooms.

A vine base was covered with bags of potpourri, with dried flowers and ribbons filling in the bare spots.

Through the centuries the shapes and forms of wreaths have done a lot of changing, so the innovative designs of the pressed flower wreaths in this chapter shouldn't surprise you. The wreaths are made by tracing a light outline of a plate or dish onto a sheet of matte board, and then arranging an assortment of pressed flowers and foliage into the wreath shape. Don't follow the penciled circle too rigidly — instead allow the curves and shapes of the pressed material to form their own design. The fluffy end of a paintbrush is ideal for moving the flowers around while your design is still in the experimental stage, and will prevent the delicate material from breaking or shattering. When you're satisfied with the design, adhere the materials with white glue.

Pressing techniques vary, but the simple method of placing the material between sheets of absorbent paper and then inserting them between the pages of a thick book for six to ten weeks usually yields good results. For thicker flowers and foliage, it may be necessary to weight the book with bricks or other heavy objects. For greater design options, try removing some of the petals and pressing them separately.

The wreath to the left is a brilliant mixture of Queen Anne's lace, silver king artemisia leaves, bee balm, salvia, statice tatarica, and salvia claryssa. The design is both delicate and formal with its exciting use of symmetry, variety, and texture. To give the wreath its final bright touch the wreath-maker used a selection of small green leaves.

Plants & Flowers That Press Well

With practice and patience you can get good pressing results with almost every type of plant and flower. For plants with three-dimensional seed heads, though, you may have to strip the petals off and press them separately.

Some plants that press particularly well are:

Wildflowers, such as Queen Anne's lace, clover, goldenrod, morning glory, and yarrow.

Herbs, such as salvia and mint.

Annuals, such as marigold, zinnia, everlastings, dianthus, and violet.

Greens, such as ferns and leaves and grasses of the flowers and shrubs mentioned above.

Pressed flower wreaths have all the charm and beauty of traditional wreaths. Note the bow designed with flowers.

Pressed Flowers

Below left, large flowers and leaves give this wreath its dynamic character.

Below right, the petals from zinnias were dried separately and then combined with dried coreopsis, celosia, and silver king artemisia leaves.

The wreath to the left below is very contemporary in its use of color and shape and yet has a deep respect for the traditions of pressed flower wreaths. The bright yellow statice sinuata, dark red geranium, bright orange coreopsis and the lavender xeranthemum in the foreground are made more brilliant with the use of subdued cream-colored Queen Anne's lace and grey artemisia stelleriana. The use of a dark background helps to bring the color of this wreath forward into view.

The wreath to the right below is a simple yet effective composition created primarily from bright zinnia (yellow) and coreopsis (orange) petals. The delicate grey details are created using silver king artemisia leaves and red celosia.

The wreath to the right has a delicate Victorian aura. We can imagine seeing this composition in a small country cottage. It is made from red salvia, yarrow leaves, statice latifolia, fleabane and Pycnanthemum pilosum. This wreath could have used small fern fronds in place of the yarrow leaves to obtain a similar look.

Right, the vibrancy of red salvia merges with the softness of statice latifolia, fleabane, yarrow leaves and Pycnanthemum virginiaum.

Wreath Whimsies

A painter's whimsy created this painted wreath which easily fits in the space between a storm door and an outside door.

Making wreaths doesn't have to be a serious, artistic process. The wreaths shown here were all made in the spirit of fun, so don't be afraid you'll get too carried away and make an ugly wreath. As long as you forestall using the glue gun or wire until you're satisfied with the results, the wreath can easily be disassembled. Go ahead — you've got nothing to lose!

Painting a wreath opens up a whole new range of possibilities. (This wreath is flat enough to fit in the space between a storm and outside door, whereas a regular wreath would get crushed.) If you like this design, feel free to copy it, or you can create your own. The base was cut with a sabre saw from plywood, and then treated with a wood sealer. The design was sketched directly onto the base, painted with acrylic paints, and the finished product was then sprayed with clear varnish. If you doubt your artistic talents, substitute plastic flower decals for painted flowers, stenciled flowers, or make a montage of floral photos clipped from magazines.

Pink flamingos set the tone for this fun wreath made from plastic lawn ornaments, silk flowers, and a ribbon-wrapped base.

Here's where the real fun begins! Plastic flamingo lawn ornaments were wired to a ribbon-wrapped reinforced styrofoam base. Adam's rib (palm) cane spirals, hens and chicks, silk orchids, and iridescent glass baubles were attached with wooden picks and then reinforced with hot glue. This high-kitsch wreath would make a great gift for a friend with discriminating taste — all in the spirit of fun, of course.

A wreath makes the perfect showcase for any collected item. Here an assortment of seldom-worn (but still precious to the owner) jewelry was attached to a straw base with floral pins.

If your jewelry box is overflowing with seldom-worn pieces, here's a fun way to put them back in use. Jewelry that's broken, out of style, or even those passed-on mementos from Aunt Louise make an interesting wreath. A small straw base (we chose a small base because the jewelry can become quite heavy) was wrapped in ribbon and the items were randomly attached with floral pins. But don't let you imagination stop here. Any small collected items — empty perfume bottles, for example — can be hot-glued to a base with pieces of jewelry tucked in to fill the crevices.

From how many family outings have you returned with a bag of shells, driftwood, feathers, and such? If you're like most people, you probably have a junk drawer somewhere in your home filled with these mementos. Or maybe the items sit on a shelf for a while and then get removed to the trash can. Well, here's a fun way to start an ongoing collection of nature's treasures. Because this wreath usually gets quite heavy, the 28-inch (71-cm.) base was reinforced with a metal ring, which also helped maintain the vine's shape. Lighter items were added with tape-covered wire and hot glue, while a basket was wired into the bottom of the base to hold the heavier items.

Each member of the family
contributed mementos
from a weekend camping
trip to decorate this vine
base. As more "natural
wonders" are found on
later trips they, too,
can be added.

This scrap fabric wreath is a great way to use up those scraps of yarn, ribbon, and fabric cluttering up your sewing area. Four layers of foam core™ were glued together to form the base after they'd been cut in the wreath shape. The first piece was cut to a 20-inch (51-cm.) diameter, while each of the next three pieces was cut ¼-inch (½-cm.) smaller in diameter to produce a staggered effect. This staggering in ring sizes gives the wreath a much fuller look. (A store-bought foam base could also have been used, with the resulting wreath being "rounder.") The fabric scraps were cut to 1 inch by 1 inch (2½ cm.) and 2 inches by 2 inches (5 cm.), while the ribbon lengths vary from 2 to 5 inches (5 - 13 cm.). Yarn scraps were also added, in lengths of 3 to 6 inches (8 - 15 cm.). The fabric and ribbon scraps were glued on individually, from the inside outward; while the yarn scraps were glued on in bunches of four to ten.

The elements are glue-gunned from the inside outward. A child old enough to wield a glue gun can easily make this wreath alone, or a younger child could help by handing you the pieces as they're glued on. If you decide to hang this wreath in your sewing area, consider adding some of your favorite colors of sewing thread to the wreath with wooden picks. When the picks are inserted at an angle, the spools easily slide off and on. Other easily lost sewing items, such as spare sewing machine needles, can be added to the wreath for safe refuge.

The hat wreath used a small, purchased crocheted hat as a base for embellishment. Dried German statice was attached with a glue gun or craft glue, with attention to keeping all the statice going in the same direction. Dried roses and larkspur, along with tiny bows, were then glued to the statice. A crocheted doily would work equally well, using safety pins instead of glue to attach the flowers.

A small crocheted hat made from a discarded doily and spray starch made a fun base for an arrangement of dried flowers.

Bags of old fabric scraps can be transformed into a decorative wreath for your sewing area. The fabric, yarn, and ribbon scraps were glue-gunned to the base.

Childhood Mementos

A child's discarded wooden alphabet blocks and the remnants of some favorite Christmas tree ornaments were glued into a wreath of pine, fir, and baby's breath.

If there's a special child in your life, you've undoubtedly looked at those inevitable accumulations of toys and wondered how to keep the memories from slipping away. Or maybe you're a grandparent who long ago packed those memories into boxes and put them in the back of a closet or in a dusty attic. Preserving those childhood relics (and all the memories that go with them) can be inexpensive and simple — just make them into wreaths.

The wreaths shown here should give you some good ideas for making your own toy wreaths. These wreaths are one of the safest ways to preserve a child's collection of small items, such as race cars or finger puppets, plus they make a nice decorative touch to a child's bedroom. (Remember to hang the wreath securely out of reach of little hands, though.) Because the items in these wreaths are so cherished, they make great Christmas or birthday gifts for far-away relatives. Adding a small portrait of the child in a light-weight frame makes the gift even more special. Hint: if your stash of toys isn't what it should be, try raiding Christmas tree ornaments for toy drummers, choo choo trains, and other childlike elements.

The wreath to the left was made from wooden tree ornaments and took less than an hour to make. Clumps of silk fir and pine were picked into small cubes of styrofoam which were then hot glued onto an 18-inch (46-cm.) straw base. A piece of styrofoam was then cut to fit one-third of the size of the hole in the wreath's center. The ornaments and blocks were glued onto this piece of foam, along with more clumps of pine and fir. The baby's breath was held together with taped floral wire and inserted into the

styrofoam with 2½-inch (6-cm.) wooden picks. A cotton printed ribbon and streamers were the final touch.

The wreath to the right started with a 14-inch (36-cm.) styrofoam base (a straw base would also work) to which plastic greenery was hot glued. Small pine cones, wooden alphabet blocks, and a plastic toy bathtub were then hot-glued amongst the greenery. The small teddy bears were attached with Velcro™, making them easily attached and removed by children. The shopping bag of teddy bears was tied on to the wreath with raffia. This wreath would be a nice centerpiece for a child's birthday celebration, with each attendee getting a teddy bear to remember the occasion.

Teddy bears (or any other favorite collection of toys) are easily attached to a straw base covered with greenery.

Fabric Wreaths

Some people enjoy working a sewing machine more than wielding a glue gun, and for them we have some ideas to convert those accumulated bags of scrap fabric into beautiful wreaths. Our wreaths were made with applique, patchwork, and lace, but don't let your imagination stop there. Any special handwork skill you have — embroidery, crewel work, or cross stitch — can be used to make completely original wreaths.

To create this wreath, a simple patchwork was made from odd scraps of fabric, and then, with pleated seam binding, made into a wreath that is both fun to look at and right at home in a country setting.

The wreath opposite right was appliqued. The applique was first done on a piece of white muslin fabric after the shape of the wreath had been outlined with chalk. (Do not cut the background fabric until after you have finished the appliqueing.) When the applique was done, a similar-sized piece of fabric was cut out — either in the same background fabric or in a color from the applique —leaving a ⅜″ (1-cm.) seam allowance. Then sew up the sides, using a piece of contrasting seam binding, until you are about 3 inches (8-cm.) from completing the side seam. Fill with shredded foam or other stuffing, and complete the seam.

This same procedure was used for the patchwork wreath, lower left: a section of pieced fabric replaces the appliqued portion, and a pleated seam binding was used. A simple bow added just the right touch. For quilting aficionados, a more complicated patchwork can be pieced and then complemented with machine or hand quilting.

A lace wreath is just an example of what can be done with various fabrics and materials. In this example, a 3-foot (1-m.) piece of lace was put onto a single length of wire. (A wire coat hanger painted white would have worked just as well.) The lace is skewed in a zig-zag fashion. Small embellishments were added, in addition to a narrow section of ribbon. Other kinds and sizes of ribbon work well, as does finely pleated fabric, which twists to create interesting visual patterns.

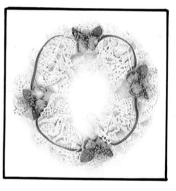

There are a myriad of ways to create wreaths using lace and ribbon. This small wreath could have been the model for a much larger wreath, combining various laces, colors, and types of ribbon.

A traditional flower pattern is appliqued here onto a piece of muslin and then transformed into a festive wreath equally at home on the wall or on a couch or chair.

Wearable Wreaths

A straw hat makes a unique base for silk flowers, clumps of moss, and a bow.

In Latin, "corona" means both wreath and crown. And, indeed, wreaths have been worn majestically throughout history. Those who participated in the Jewish Feast of the Tabernacle wore wreaths, as did the Olympians of Ancient Greece, who wore wreaths of wild leaves, pine, parsley, or laurel. As a mockery of the traditionally worn wreath, Jesus was made to wear a crown (wreath) of thorns. Crowns of flowers also became halos of Christian saints and martyrs. A crown of gold laurel leaves bedecked the head of Napoleon, and all the crowns of England were originally wreaths.

The wreaths pictured here are certainly not as majestic as those of history. In fact, they're mostly for fun. And, when you're not wearing them, keep in mind that they still look great hung on the wall.

The head wreath opposite right is especially nice for brides and makes a long-lasting keepsake after the wedding day. Clumps of German statice, baby's breath, larkspur, and statice were wired to a custom-fitted wire base covered with green floral tape. Streams of ribbon were then added to match the gown or complement the flowers.

An ordinary straw hat becomes a fun, wearable wreath, left, when decorated with flowers and a bow. The silk flowers — baby's breath and pink carnations — were attached to the hat with hot glue, and small clumps of moss were tucked in as filler. The bow was tied around the hat's base and then secured with a well-hidden safety pin.

Right, a bridal wreath to keep as an heirloom was made from dried flowers wired to a custom-fitted wire base.

Wearable Wreaths

Leftover scraps of moss and vine were made into miniature bases and then adorned with dried flowers, vegetables, and ribbons.

This assortment of wreath jewelry is both fun to make and fun to wear. The pin backings were purchased from a craft store and glued to the backs of small (2- to 3½-inch; 5- to 9-cm.) moss and grapevine bases. The flowers and ribbons can be stuck in individually with small picks or glued on. These wreaths take only 15 minutes or so to make and are a great way to use up leftover materials.

making & using bows

A bow is a symmetrical arrangement of ribbon loops with or without streamers, tied securely at the center. The number of loops, the size of the loops, and the size of the ribbon will determine the look of the bow.

Here, you'll learn to make a basic bow suitable for a wreath. It uses a medium width ribbon, about 1 inch wide (2½-cm.) that would be appropriate for a wreath about 10 - 14 inches (25 - 36-cm.) wide.

The wreath is made by creating a streamer and then constructing two medium-length loops, two long loops, two short loops and finishing up with two medium-length loops.

1. Cut, at an angle, an 8-inch (20-cm.) length of ribbon. This will be the first streamer.

2. Crimp the middle of the streamer and hold it tightly between the thumb and index finger.

3. Using a spool of ribbon, create a third streamer by crimping the ribbon about the same distance (4 inches, 10 cm.) from the end of the ribbon as the other streamers.

4. Keeping streamers held firmly, form a medium-sized loop, about 3 - 4 inches (8 - 10 cm.) long, taking care to keep the good side facing out. A loop actually involves gathering a top loop and a bottom loop.

5. Repeat Step 4, making another medium-sized loop. Note that the loops are not built on top of each other. Rather, they are made side-by-side. Keep the center tightly crimped.

6. Create two longer loops, about 1 inch (2½ cm.) longer than the medium length loops in the same manner as above, making sure to place them aside the medium-sized streamers.

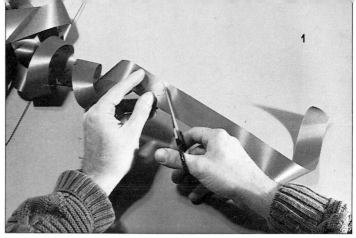

7. Create two smaller loops - about an inch (2½ cm.) smaller than the medium-sized loops on top of (not beside) the larger loops, holding them tightly between the thumb and index finger. (At this point, you can add a small single loop, made by wrapping the ribbon around your finger and placing the loop on top of the center of the smaller loops, to cover the wire that will hold the bow together, see below.)

8. Add two more medium-length loops beside, not on top of, the long loops.

9. Switch the bow from one hand to the other, holding the crimped ribbon tightly. Be careful, this is probably the trickiest part of the whole procedure.

10. Pull out and cut the ribbon about the same length as a medium loop and cut at an angle with scissors.

11. Adjust the angle of the cut if desired to match that of the original streamers.

12. Slip a length of florist wire under your thumb and fold it in half and twist it around the streamers and loops. If you have made a small finger loop, be sure the wire goes through the middle of this loop.

13. Pulling the bow up, twist the wire to secure the bow. Now you can relax your hands. The work is done.

14. Fluff and straighten out the bow by pulling the streamers and rolling your finger around the inside of the loops in the order in which they were gathered.

15. To attach the bow to a wreath, twist the wire around the wreath base or attach the bow to a wooden floral pick and insert into the base.

The style of your bow can be changed by using thicker or thinner ribbon widths.

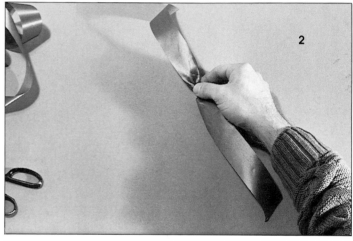

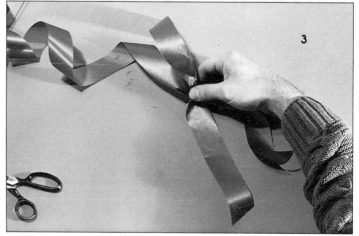

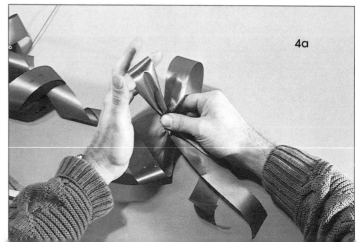

4b

5a

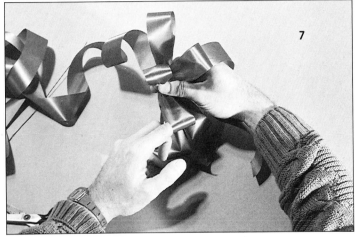

7

5b

8

6a

9

10a

13

10b

14a

11

14b

12

14c

Most wreaths will not last forever, but with a little care, the quality and length of their lifetime can be expanded considerably.

1. Sunlight and moisture damage wreaths made with dried materials, so choose your hanging locations with care.
2. Wreaths made of delicate dried materials can be cleaned with the tip of a feather or a paint brush. Wreaths with sturdier dried materials can be given a light dusting using a hair dryer on its cold air setting. (Hold the dryer at least a foot away from your wreath.)
3. The sheen of glycerined materials can be restored with a damp cloth.
4. When not in use, store your wreaths in loose paper bags in a dry location. (Plastic bags will cause condensation.)
5. Wreaths made from nuts and cones should be sprayed with a protective layer of polyurethane, shellac, or even hairspray.

wielding a glue gun

Wreathmaking mania is a common malaise among even novice wreathmakers. And once you've made even a small commitment to the art of wreathmaking, the first thing you should buy is a glue gun. They're available in a variety of formats, from simple to complex, and under a variety of brand names. Some cheaper (but no less effective) models require you to manually push the dry glue sticks into the back of the barrel to melt the glue. The pressure you apply to the end of the glue stick then determines the flow of the glue. Other, more sophisticated models have a trigger mechanism that allows you to insert the dry glue sticks and then control your glue coverage by pulling a trigger.

The advantages of a glue gun are many: precise application, quick drying, and good adhesion. The disadvantage is that when the hot glue gets on your hands — and it will —you'll utter profanities you didn't know you knew. Some wreathmakers take the precaution of wearing gloves, although they can be restrictive and uncomfortable. Our advice is to have a bowl of cold water strategically placed on your worktable. You can usually cool the glue before the first expletive is out of your mouth.

Another disadvantage is the mess. There's almost no human way to keep a glue gun neat. Since the guns have a tendency to drool when you're not looking, we suggest you keep a piece of cardboard nearby to rest your glue gun on when not in use. Also, keep the area under your wreath well padded with plastic or newspaper. When your wreath is finished, be sure to check for hair-like strands of glue that often form between your hands and the wreath.

CHALLAH WREATH

(Makes one 15 inch (38-cm.) Wreath)

STEP ONE INGREDIENTS:
- 1 cup Lukewarm Water
- 1/3 cup Honey (Clover honey is best)
- 1 pkg. Active Dry Yeast (1-1½ tbs.)
- 1 1/3 cup Unbleached Bread Flour

STEP TWO INGREDIENTS:
- 1/3 cup Light Salad Oil
- 1/2 tbs. Salt
- 2 Large Eggs (beaten)
- 3 1/3 cup Unbleached Bread Flour

WASH INGREDIENTS:
- 1 Egg
- 1 tsp. Milk
- 1/4 cup Raisins (optional)

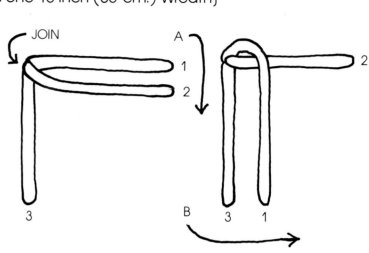

STEP ONE — Making the Sponge

In a large bowl, combine the ingredients. Stir until all ingredients are wet and there are no large lumps. Cover with a towel. Place in a warm place and allow to "rise" until doubled in bulk.

STEP TWO — Making the Dough

Add oil, salt and beaten eggs to the sponge and beat until thoroughly mixed and the batter is smooth.

Add 3 cups of the flour (reserve the remaining flour) until the batter is too stiff to stir.

NOTE: If you are using a home mixer with a dough hook, add flour until the dough forms a ball on the hook and cleans the side of the bowl. Knead at low-to-medium speed for seven minutes.

Turn the dough out onto a lightly floured surface and knead until the dough is smooth and elastic (7-10 minutes) using reserved flour sparingly to keep the dough from sticking to the surface.

STEP THREE — Proofing the Dough

Place the kneaded dough in a lightly greased bowl. Cover. Place in a warm place and allow to rise until doubled in bulk (About 1 hour, depending on temperature).

STEP FOUR — Shaping the Wreath

Remove a lump of dough the size of a golf ball and set aside.

Divide the dough into three pieces of approximately equal weight. Roll each piece into a "snake" about 3/4" (2-cm.) in diameter and 30" to 36" (76 - 91 cm.) in length.

NOTE: These pieces must be equal in length. Join the strands as shown.

Braid from outside of the double strand maintaining the right-angle arrangement of the pieces. The dough strands should be braided somewhat loosely to allow for expansion. When completed, press the ends of the strands together to close the braid.

NOTE: This process requires a large open surface.

On a large baking sheet, form the braid into a circle, allowing the dough to lie flat without being stretched. Join the two ends very firmly.

Roll the golf ball-sized piece of dough into a snake about 1/4" (1/2-cm.) in diameter and 12 - 14" (31 - 36 cm.) long. Form into a bow over the spot where you joined the braid. Press at the joint of the bow to join with the wreath.

OPTIONAL: Press a raisin into each joint of the braid.

STEP FIVE: Rising and Baking

Cover the wreath and set aside to rise until almost doubled in bulk. Mix the egg-milk wash. When the dough has risen, gently brush on the egg wash, covering the entire wreath. Place in a pre-heated 350° F (177° C) oven and bake until the top is golden brown and the sides are no longer soft to the touch.

When done, carefully slide the wreath from pan onto a cooling rack. Cool thoroughly.

Dick Gilbert
The Stone Soup
Asheville, North Carolina   U.S.A.

Nomenclature conforms to Bailey's Hortes Third

A

ACROCLINIUM .... Helipterum roseum
AMARANTH .... Amaranthus
ANNUAL STATICE .... Limonium sinuatum
APPLE ....: Malus pumila
ARBORVITAE .... Thuja
ARTEMISIA .... Artemisia ludoviciana
ASTILBE .... Astilbe chinensis

B

BABY'S BREATH .... Gypsophila paniculata
BAMBOO .... Arundinaria
BAY .... Laurus nobilis
BEE BALM .... Monarda didyma
BITTERSWEET .... Celastrus scandens
BLACK-EYED SUSAN .... Rudbeckia serotina
BLUE SPRUCE .... Picea pungens
BORAGE .... Borago
BOXWOOD .... Buxus sempervirens
BUCKEYE .... Aesculus glabra

C

CANDYTUFT .... Iberis saxatilis
CARROT .... Daucus carota
CASPIA .... Limonium caspia
CATNIP .... Nepeta cataria
CEDAR .... Cedrus
CELANDINE .... Chelidonium majus
CELOSIA .... Celosia cristata
CHESTNUT .... Castanea vesca
CHIVE .... Allium schoenoprasum
CINNAMON (wild) .... Canella winterana
CLEMATIS .... Clematis (sp.)
CLOVER .... Trifolium
COCKSCOMB ...... Celosia argentea cristata
CONEFLOWER .... Echinacea
CORNFLOWER .... Centaurea cyanus
COREOPSIS .... Coreopsis
COTTON .... Gossypium
CYPRESS .... Cupressus (sp.)

D

DAFFODIL .... Narcissus pseudo narcissus
DELPHINIUM .... Delphinium hybrids
DOGWOOD .... Cornus

E

ELSHOLTZIA .... Elsholtzia strauntonii
ENGLISH IVY .... Hedera helix
EUCALYPTUS .... Eucalyptus cinerea

F

FEVERFEW .... Chrysanthemum parthenium
FIR .... Abies

G

GARLIC .... Allium sativum
GERANIUM .... Pelargonium
GERMANDER .... Teucrium
GERMAN STATICE .... Lilmonium tatarica
GLOBE AMARANTH ...... Gomphrena globosa
GOAT'S RUE .... Galega officinalis
GOLDENROD .... Solidago canadensis
GOMPHRENA .... Gomphrena globosa
GOURD .... Cucurbits
GRAPE (vine) .... Vitis
GROUND PINE .... Lycopodium obscurum

H

HAWTHORNE (berry) .... Crataegus
HEATHER .... Calluna
HEMLOCK .... Tsuga canadensis
HOLLY .... Ilex
HONESTY .... Lunaria annua
HONEY-LOCUST .... Gleditsia
HOREHOUND .... Marrubium vulgare
HOT PEPPER .... Capsicum annuum
HYDRANGEA .... Hydrangea

I

INDIAN CORN .... Zea mays
IRONWEED .... Veronia (sp.)
IVY .... Hedera

J

JUNIPER .... Juniperus

L

LAMB'S EAR .... Stachys lanata
LARKSPUR .... Delphinium
LAUREL .... Prunus laurocerasus
LAVENDER .... Lavandula angustifolia

M

MAGNOLIA .... Magnolia grandiflora
MALLOW .... Althea officinalis
MARGUERITE, Golden ...... Anthemis tinctoria
MARIGOLD .... Tagetes (sp.)
MINT .... Mentha
MISTLETOE .... Phoradendron serotinum
MORNING GLORY .... Ipomaea
MOUNTAIN MINT .... Pycnanthemum
MUSHROOM .... Fungi
MYRTLE .... Myrtus communis

N

NIGELLA .... Nigella damascena

O

OAK .... Quercus
OKRA .... Hibiscus esculentus
ONION .... Allium
ORCHID .... Orchidaceae
OREGANO .... Origanum compacta

P

PALM .... Palmae
PARSLEY .... Petroselinum
PEARLY EVERLASTING .... Anaphalis
PEONY .... Paeonia lactiflora

P   continued

PINE .... Pinus
PINON .... Edulis
PIN OAK .... Quercus palustris
PITCHER PLANT .... Sarracenia
POTATO .... Solanun tuberosum
POT MARIGOLD .... Calendula officinalis
PROTEA .... Proteaceae
PUSSY WILLOW .... Salix discolor

Q

QUEEN ANNE'S LACE .... Daucus carota

R

RAFFIA .... Raphia ruffia
RED CLOVER .... Trifolium pratense
REDWOOD .... Sequoia sempervirens
REED .... Phragmites communis
ROSE HIP .... Rosa rugosa
ROSEMARY .... Rosmarinus officinalis
RUE .... Ruta graveolens
RYE .... Secale cereale

S

SAFFLOWER .... Carthamus tinctorius
SAGE .... Salvia officinalis
SANDALWOOD .... Santalum album
SANTOLINA .... Santolina chamaecyparissus
SARRACENIA LILY .... Saraceniaceae
SAVORY .... Satureja
SCABIOSA .... Scabiosa stellata
SCOTCH BROOM .... Cytisus scoparius
SELF-HEAL .... Prunella vulgaris
SEQUOIA .... Taxodiaceae
SILVER KING ARTEMESIA ...... Aretmesia albula
SORREL .... Rumex
SOUTHERNWOOD ...... Artemisia arbrotanum
SPANISH MOSS .... Tillandsia usneoides
SPHAGNUM MOSS .... Sphagnum (sp.)
STAR FLOWER .... Stachys grandiflora
STATICE .... Limonium
STRAWFLOWER .... Helichrysum
SUGAR BUSH .... Protea mellifera
SUNFLOWER .... Helianthus annuus
SWAMP IRIS .... Saraceniaceae
SWEET GUM .... Liquidambar styraciflua
SWEET WOODRUFF .... Asperula

T

TANSY .... Tanacetum vulgare
TARRAGON .... Artemisia dracunculus
THYME .... Thymus vulgaris
TOBACCO .... Nicotiana
TREE FERN .... Dicksonia (sp.)
TULIP .... Tulipa

V

VERONICA .... Spicata
VERBENA .... Verbena
VIOLET .... Viola

W

WHEAT .... Triticum aestivum
WISTERIA .... Wisteria frutescens
WORMWOOD .... Artemisia absinthium

Y

YARROW .... Achillea
YUCCA .... Yucca

Z

ZINNIA .... Zinnia elegans

index

acknowledgements

Contributing Designers:

Juliane Bronder (pages 42, 70, 71, 74-bottom, 74-top, 75, 102-left, 103, 105, 110, 111, 127) received her floral design training at the American Floral Art School in Chicago, Illinois. She now teaches floral design and sells her works in her own store, the Floral Design Studio in Asheville, North Carolina.

A Christmas House (pages 55, 56, 58, 59, 60, 90/91, 123, 128, 129) located in Hendersonville and Asheville, North Carolina sells and creates holiday wreaths throughout the year.

Fred Tyson Gaylor (pages 46, 49, 50/51, 54, 66, 68, 69, 72/73, 116-top, 122, 125) earned his B.A. in Creative Art at the University of North Carolina, and his M.A. in Adult Education at East Carolina University. He enjoys discovering unconventional ways to use conventional wreathmaking materials. He also enjoys painting special effect scenes for movie sets.

Cynthia Gillooly (pages 4, 53, 67, 101, 102, 109, 112, 134) and **Gary Leidner** (pages 61, 95, 96, 97, 98, 113) are partners in the Golden Cricket, a floral design studio in Asheville, North Carolina. Their wreaths favor naturally dried materials but they're always looking for innovative ideas. Cynthia has been in floral design for eight years and Gary is a hair designer by profession.

Gail Martin (pages 48, 76, 77-top, 77-bottom, 81-bottom, 104, 115, 133) creates her dried and fresh flower wreaths in her flower and antique store, Celebration, in Asheville, North Carolina. Gail recycles flowers from her fresh arrangements by hanging them upside down to dry. She has a particular fondness for roses.

Sandy Mush Herb Nursery (pages 40, 41-bottom, 41-top, 47, 78, 79, 80, 81-top, 82, 84, 85, 87, 88, 89, 92, 93, 94, 106, 116-bottom, 117, 135-bottom and top) is the full-time passion of Kate Jayne and Fairman Jayne and their children, Nicketie and Christopher. They grow an extensive variety of culinary, decorative, and fragrant herbs which they sell, along with their wreaths, through their mail order catalog and The Herbal Handbook. (Route 2, Surrett Cove Road, Leicester, N.C. U.S.A. 28748)

Claudette Stewart (pages 52, 99, 114, 116-bottom, 118, 120-left, 120-right, 121) divides her time between wreathmaking and operating Yellow Mountain Flower Farm with her two sons. She grows all the ingredients for her dried flower and pressed flower wreaths which she sells at craft fairs.

Also Thanks To:

Richard Faulkner (page 125)

Dick Gilbert (page 100)

Olivia Henry (pages 130-right, 132)

Pat Jewsbury (pages 44-bottom, 45)

Kit Meckly (pages 64, 65)

Jeanne Pulleyn (pages 130-left, 131)

Micah Pulleyn (pages 39, 126)

Sue Spiegal (page 57)

Skip Skeppe (page 107)

Beth Stickle (page 124)

Tommy Wolffe (pages 42/43-top, 43 44-top, 63)